Books by Norman Zierold

THE CHILD STARS

LITTLE CHARLIE ROSS

THREE SISTERS IN BLACK

THREE
SISTERS
IN BLACK

Mary Snead, Caroline Martin, and Virginia Wardlaw, the three sisters, as sketched in court by a newspaper artist.

NORMAN ZIEROLD

THREE
SISTERS
IN BLACK

with illustrations

LITTLE, BROWN AND COMPANY · BOSTON · TORONTO

*Published simultaneously in Canada
by Little, Brown & Company (Canada) Limited*

PRINTED IN THE UNITED STATES OF AMERICA

For Edith Bel Geddes and Bert Marino,
friends dear to my heart

THREE
SISTERS
IN BLACK

1

To stargazers on the Eastern seaboard, November 27, 1909, was memorable for a total eclipse of the moon, which shrouded the night in densest black. For inhabitants of East Orange, New Jersey, then a quiet residential suburb of New York, the darkness later seemed a sinister omen, an angry augury. The next day, Sunday, remained cool and gray. On Monday afternoon, November 29, a telephone call pierced the small-town stillness, opening one of the most macabre crime mysteries in modern times.

At 388 Main Street, East Orange police headquarters, Sergeant Timothy Caniff picked up the receiver. He noted the time as 4:40 P.M. At the other end of the line a woman's voice, soft and cultivated, asked whether a coroner could be sent immediately to her house. There had been "an accident." The sergeant explained that the county had no coroner's office; he would send out a physician. The soft voice gave an address, 89 North Fourteenth Street, and hung up. Unable to reach the county physician, Caniff called his assistant, Herbert M. Simmons. Dr. Simmons walked to the designated location from his nearby office, crossing the Lackawanna Railroad overpass, then continuing three short blocks on North Fourteenth Street before reaching number 89, a cheerless gray frame house of two stories topped by an attic.

Medical satchel in hand, he was climbing the porch steps when the front door opened. Before him stood a tall spare woman dressed all in black, a long cape flowing to the ground, heavy veils secreting the face. Startled by this somber apparition, the physician was relieved to hear the pleasing accents of the South in the voice that beckoned to him.

"Please come in," it said. "I am Virginia Wardlaw."

Simmons identified himself. Silently, the woman in black led him up a flight of stairs and down the second-floor hallway. Open doors along the way gave no sign of occupancy. At the end of the hall, the woman halted. Simmons hesitated, knowing he was about to see what he had come for, the intractable face of death.

For the physician it was an everyday experience, and yet one to which he was never fully reconciled. Steeling himself, he turned the knob, pushed the door, saw that he had entered the bathroom. There it was, the nude body of a young woman in the small, half-filled bathtub. The slender figure was in a crouching position, legs doubled up at the knees, the left hand lightly grasping a washcloth, the head submerged in the cold bath water and tipped slightly to the right, directly under the faucet. Long auburn hair streamed like a fan on the water. The physician gently raised the head and saw a face that must in life have been very beautiful — each feature fine and classically formed, dominated by large brown eyes now fixed in a sightless stare.

After a preliminary inspection of the body, Simmons's attention shifted to a pile of clothing on the floor. To one of the garments a note was pinned. The physician read the bold clear handwriting:

Last year my little daughter died; other near and dear ones have gone before. I have been prostrated with illness for a long time. When you read this I will have committed suicide. Do not grieve over me. Rejoice with me that death

*brings a blessed relief from pain and suffering greater than I
can bear.*

O. W. M. SNEAD

"Who is this woman?" Simmons asked the veiled figure in
the doorway.

"She is my niece, Ocey Snead. She has been despondent
since her first child died last year. Then her husband died
seven months ago. She also has a four-month-old son who is
ill in St. Christopher's Hospital in Brooklyn. She herself has
been in very poor health."

"When did you find the body?"

"Only a short time before I called the police station."

At this reply, the physician looked up sharply. He tried to
control his voice so that accusation would not enter: "But
this woman has been dead fully twenty-four hours."

"Well, perhaps she has," answered Virginia Wardlaw. "The
truth of the matter is, she asked me yesterday afternoon to
start a fire in the kitchen range to heat water for her bath.
She was about to take a nap. I started a fire and then, having
business to attend to, went away, leaving her to sleep undis-
turbed."

"Were you two living alone in this house?"

"Yes."

"And in twenty-four hours you never made inquiry, never
went to see how she was when she didn't appear at meals
or before bedtime?"

"She had asked not to be disturbed, did I not tell you?"

"The rooms in this house seem empty. Why are you living
like this? Why haven't you any furniture, or any comforts?"

"It has suited us to live this way. We had only settled here
temporarily."

Despite his efforts to appear casual, Simmons's tone had
become increasingly challenging; that of his interlocutor had

grown cold, almost disdainful. Virginia Wardlaw refused to reply at all to further questioning and asked the physician to complete his business as swiftly as possible. On leaving, Simmons noted again the empty rooms, the lack of heat in the cold, bleak house. At the nearest telephone he called the police station, reporting the case as an apparent suicide but with suspicious elements that warranted sending a detective.

An hour had passed since the original call to the Main Street station. It was nearing six o'clock and night had fallen when Sergeant William H. O'Neill knocked at number 89. The curtains were drawn. It appeared that a dim gas lamp burned within. When the door opened the woman in black stood framed in the entranceway, demanding to know the sergeant's business. He had been ordered to inspect the premises, he explained. In caustic tones, she said she did not understand why, then turned and led the way upstairs. In the bathroom, O'Neill saw the body and read the suicide note. He asked to see the rest of the house.

The tour started with the attic. It was completely empty. Returning to the second floor, O'Neill thrust his head first into one room, then into a second, and a third. Each was empty, with only a silk maternity gown in a closet bearing mute witness to the life that had ebbed away. A fourth small room opened over the porch. In it stood the narrow cot which had been the dead girl's last bed. By the pillow O'Neill found a locket containing the photo of a smiling baby. Two pins held a tag which read: *Lock of David Snead's first hair Aug. 18,'09.* On the floor lay a pair of dainty shoes and a fine black silk gown, evidence of onetime affluence; also a broadcloth coat with silver lining and white silk facings on the lapels. Near the cot was a barrel covered with a white cloth. Combs and hairpins indicated it had been used as a makeshift dressing table. On a box in the corner stood a package of cereal and empty cans that had

contained evaporated milk. Bits of oranges and orange peel-
ings were scattered around the room. The only element of
decoration to relieve the pathetic squalor was a painting
of a ballerina on one wall.

Bare floors rang hollow to O'Neill's tread as he made his
way through the house, the shrouded figure in black following silently, her sepulchral aspect made more sinister by the
dim gaslight. In the downstairs hall a chair missing front
legs was propped on an ordinary soapbox; piled on it were
embroidered coverlets that might once have graced a divan.
The parlor was bare save for a corner stand holding a soli-
tary umbrella. In the dining room the table consisted of a
packing box with an improvised plank top. A lone chair had
been fashioned by nailing a willow chair-back to a dry goods
box. A closet contained a large quantity of cheap un-
bleached muslin which had evidently been used to blanket
windows in the house. The gloomy kitchen was dirty and
unkempt; morsels of food lay strewn about. Finally, in the
cellar a heater of ancient vintage was hopelessly out of repair, with not even an ash of coal remaining.

Tragedy seemed to be in the very atmosphere of the
house, symbolized by the black raiment of its only remaining
occupant, Virginia Wardlaw, to whom O'Neill now addressed himself, standing facing her, for neither of the
makeshift chairs seemed adequate for sitting. The detective
regretted the stiffness, the discomfort of thus confronting
her. His observance of her movements had convinced him
she was elderly, perhaps close to sixty years of age. Her
mind, however, was sharp and quick. O'Neill found the answers to his questions parried adroitly. The basic story remained the one she had told Dr. Simmons: Ocey Snead had
been ill and despondent since the death of her first child,
Mary Alberta, early in 1908. The death of her husband in
March of the current year had added to her sorrows, which

seemed to have no end. Her second child, David, born in August, had been sickly and they were forced to place him in St. Christopher's Hospital in Brooklyn.

Who was Ocey Snead? What was her maiden name? Where was she born? These questions the woman in black refused to answer. What was the husband's name? Where had he died? Were there other members of the family nearby? Again, silence or evasion.

"Let me go and I will notify the girl's relatives and then return to you," the woman suggested. Her offer was refused.

"How long have you lived in East Orange?"

"Perhaps ten days."

"Why did you come here?"

"For Ocey's health. I came along to nurse her."

"For her health? To this empty house, with no heat and no furniture?"

"I have answered your question as best I could."

"There's only one cot. Where did you sleep?"

"On the floor. Must you continue asking these questions? It does not seem quite fair. By what right do you ask them?"

Detective O'Neill ignored this sally and continued his interrogation. Was it possible that two people could live together in a small house, the one sickly, the other not checking on her condition for twenty-four hours? Yes, came the reply, for Ocey had asked not to be disturbed. Had her absence not been noted at mealtime or upon retiring for the night? No, for she, Virginia, had come and gone, tending to errands. Had she not had occasion herself, in twenty-four hours, to use the bathroom? No. Had Ocey left the house during this period? She did not know.

"You've only been here ten days. Where did you live before?"

"In the Flatlands section of Brooklyn."

"Where in the Flatlands section?"

"Must you go on like this? Must I answer that?"

"I will find out eventually."

"At East 48th Street and Mill Lane. Now may I be allowed to rest?"

With his first substantial clue in hand, Sergeant O'Neill was not about to leave his quarry. To the unhappy woman before him he explained that she would have to come to the police station. She did not protest. Carrying only the small bag already in her hand, she stepped ahead of him, leaving the mournful house of death to which she would never return.

At headquarters, Chief of Police James Bell questioned the woman in black — who emphasized that she was *Miss* Virginia Wardlaw — from early evening until midnight without making any further headway. To the chief, she seemed cunning, skilled at hiding key facts. Finally, he booked her for the night as a material witness, then drove her to the Essex County Jail, fifteen minutes away on Wilsey Street in Newark. There were too many loose ends, too many unexplained circumstances. Who exactly were these people apparently of a better station in life yet surrounded by squalor? Why this secretive manner? Would a young woman in a weakened troubled condition write a suicide note in so clear, so unwavering a hand? Was the note in fact genuine? How could Ocey Snead have summoned the resolution, the strength of will to hold her face under water until death? Would not the human spirit have asserted itself, convulsively, instinctively rejecting so grim an act? Was it possible, Chief Bell asked himself, that another hand than her own, a sinister and malevolent hand, held her head under water until life slipped away?

2

BY THE END OF THE NEXT DAY, Tuesday, November 30, mounting evidence convinced Bell that foul play had occurred. In Kunz's Morgue, to which the body was removed, County Physician William H. McKenzie performed an autopsy. It confirmed that death had come to Ocey Snead by drowning in a four-foot bathtub — a sad irony was involved, for Virginia Wardlaw had explained that Ocey was short for Oceana. The autopsy also showed the body emaciated to the last degree, like that of a person suffering from starvation. It weighed only eighty pounds.

Detectives in East Orange spent a busy day. Neighbors around 89 North Fourteenth testified they seldom saw lights in any room of the house, but that on Sunday night, November 28, the entire second floor was illuminated for several hours. The shadows of several persons were seen passing to and fro behind the curtains. Then the lights went out.

Checking with the local hack company, police found cabman Frank Perrier. He recalled the day, November 14, that Ocey Snead and her aunt arrived in East Orange, their only luggage the handbags they were carrying. He had taken them the short distance from the Roseville station to 89 North Fourteenth Street. The young girl had appeared weak and ill. He had helped her into the house. Thereafter only the older woman appeared on the street, employing him to transport her to the nearby station. On Thanksgiving eve, November 24, she had asked him to take her to a good physician. From a list she presented, they had jointly selected Dr. Charles E. Teeter of 418 Orange Street. The detectives called at this address.

Teeter remembered the nocturnal visit of the woman in black. She had asked him to come with her to North Fourteenth Street for the purpose of providing a health certificate. His protests at the late hour only made her more insistent. Finally he had acquiesced, accompanying her in the cab. Once in the house, she had led him to an upstairs room where he had found a young woman. His physical examination disclosed that she was weak and inclined to bronchitis but otherwise in normal health. He signed a certificate to that effect. Before leaving he had commented on the lack of heat in the house. "Well, what of it? We are only here temporarily," the woman in black replied.

John B. Foster, a local druggist, told police he had seen Virginia Wardlaw a number of times over the last year. Each time she asked him for the names of doctors. Recently, she inquired where a convalescing woman might be comfortable and get proper medical attention. He had given her the list of doctors which she had shown the cabman. Once he made a delivery to the North Fourteenth Street house. He had not seen Ocey Snead. At the time Virginia Wardlaw accounted for the lack of furniture by saying they were "cleaning up." To the druggist, she seemed somewhat "queer."

From the office of Menzier, Mutchler and Company, rental agents, came conflicting stories. Various employees had seen both a young woman and an older, but the latter did not seem to fit the description of Virginia Wardlaw, save for the matter of wearing black. The only certain facts were that someone had first appeared on November 13, and someone had come the next day for the keys, as well as to pay rent on number 89, fourteen dollars for the last half of the month.

A restaurant owner in East Orange reported a woman in black as a regular customer in recent weeks. Her ample meals had favored oysters as a start, followed by a meat course, and then dessert.

While Chief Bell pondered the call to obtain a health certificate for Ocey Snead, and the varying identities reported by the rental agents, Detective O'Neill was off on a rich harvest of discovery. In New York a survey of hotel registers showed Virginia Wardlaw checking into the exclusive Brevoort in early August. A clerk recalled a woman in black paying for a room and leaving in a huff when it proved inadequate.

The police trail led from the fine Fifth Avenue hostelry to the Flatlands section of Brooklyn; it ended in a cheerless house at 1693 East 48th Street. Neighbors were all familiar with the two-family brick structure, which until recently had been occupied by a beautiful young girl who was ill and seldom seen, and not one, but two — some said three — older women in black. So strange were their comings and goings that area residents spoke of number 1693 as the House of Mystery.

Some of the windows had shutters, always closed. Others were draped not only with shades but with sheets of heavy muslin backed by thick blankets. The few who entered said the inside was almost totally bare, the rooms dark as the dead of night. Only at night did activity in the house usually begin, the black-draped, black-veiled figures appearing like shadows in the backyard to burn refuse, the one sometimes vanishing in a cab only to return much later, never stopping to converse with a passing neighbor. It was a dwelling which adults gazed on with morbid questioning eyes, which fearful children skirted by crossing the street.

About six weeks before, gossip had it, an auto was seen at

the front door. A tall young man got out and entered the house. He left after a few minutes and hurried away at top speed in his machine. The same auto was reportedly seen in front of the house a week later.

Living next door, Thomas Devereaux said that he and his wife often heard peculiar noises coming from the House of Mystery. They had tried to look into the back window but couldn't; weeds eight feet high cut off their view. Mrs. Val Brown, another neighbor, reported hearing constant hammerings. Even more sinister was the story of Mrs. Ethel Moore, who had assisted at the birth of Ocey Snead's second child. At the time, said Mrs. Moore, the new mother appeared weak and hungry. Several times she had cried out that she was being starved to death.

The man on the local milk delivery route told O'Neill he left eight quarts of milk each morning at the House of Mystery. The women inside, he related, always seemed afraid he might catch a glimpse of the rooms. Once, coming home late at night, he had seen the shadowy figure of Virginia Wardlaw approaching, a bundle in her arms. As he stepped in front of her she moved deftly aside, concealing the bundle under her long black cloak. Without a word she entered the house. On another occasion, to his amazement, she asked if he would use his wagon to take a "sick woman" to a sanitarium. When he suggested instead the hire of an ambulance, it seemed to frighten her and no more was said of the matter. The milk deliveries were eventually stopped because the bills went unpaid.

After listening to these stories, Sergeant O'Neill contacted George Kelly, the janitor who cared for a row of ten houses in the area. Together they inspected the premises of number 1693. They found them as bare as the East Orange dwelling, with pieces of broken furniture scattered about, odds and ends of clothing in closets, and a few canned goods and packs of dry biscuits in the kitchen. Cobwebs covered the walls and ceilings; signs of decay were everywhere.

In the downstairs hallway the two men were met by an enterprising New York *World* reporter, put on the scent by the paper's Newark agent. The reporter immediately drew O'Neill's attention to dark spots on the floor which looked like bloodstains. The spots led from the front parlor up the stairs to the second floor and along the hall to the bathroom. Returning to the ground floor, the reporter looked into the kitchen range and found a mass of yellow hair. Wrapped up in its center were two irregularly shaped bones, one of which resembled the femur, the other the skull of a young child, showing the nose bones and the socket of an eye.

Janitor Kelly provided O'Neill with the basic chronology of the house's occupancy. About a year and a half ago Ocey moved in with her husband Fletcher Snead. She was perhaps twenty-four, a beautiful if somewhat frail young lady with auburn hair parted in the middle and combed smoothly back, large soft brown eyes, and a gentle, sweet nature. Her husband was the picture of a refined Southern gentleman, with handsome, clean-cut features. They seemed happy.

Several months after their arrival, two older women dressed always in black came to live with them, followed after a time by a third, also veiled, also wearing black. In March of the current year, Fletcher Snead had left. In August, Ocey, increasingly weak, had given birth to a baby boy.

During the last year, the household was always being dispossessed; apparently they were unable to raise the twenty-five-dollar monthly rent. Each time, one of the women would contact agent Harold Moore, give her name, always different from the previous lease holder, and regain possession of number 1693. Money would suddenly be produced.

On one occasion, when the occupants were about to be evicted, a member of the trio handed Moore a hundred-dollar bill to cover matters. Last November 11 the agent finally ousted them for good. Their belongings went into storage at the Eagle Warehouse in Brooklyn, the delivery made at night. In the morning neighbors saw only barred shutters on an empty silent house.

By inquiring about, Kelly had learned that the family — the presumption was of one related unit — had at different times required the services of a doctor named Pettit and a lawyer named Fee. Followed by the *World* reporter and other journalists drawn to the scene, Sergeant O'Neill called first on Dr. William R. Pettit, whom he found at 1825 East 37th Street, Brooklyn. The young physician had vivid and startling recollections of the weird household.

Dr. Pettit had first been called in to treat Ocey Snead in the spring. Also in the house at the time were two women in black, two sisters who were aunts of the patient. On certain visits a third sister was present along with a far more aged figure, thought to be the sisters' mother. All these women must have slept on the floor, for the only cot in the house, on the second floor, was occupied by the ailing niece.

His patient, Dr. Pettit stated, was suffering from general weakness, the result of lack of nutrition and proper care. On his first visit he prescribed fresh air, a restorative diet, and medicine. On his next call he found that no effort had been made to follow his instructions. When he asked why, the woman who was probably Virginia Wardlaw told him they could not afford the prescriptions, that all their money was needed to meet premiums on the invalid's twenty thousand dollars' worth of insurance policies.

Dr. Pettit had attended Ocey Snead at the birth of her baby on August 1. When he mentioned that she might need a postnatal operation, one which could prove fatal, the two sisters present, to his astonishment, fairly jumped at the idea. The operation was performed successfully.

Ocey Snead's baby boy, named David Pollock, was born sickly, but the mother and Dr. Pettit both felt with proper care he would be all right. The women in black fed the baby condensed milk and other foods at variance with those Dr. Pettit specified. Over the mother's objections, they placed the child in St. Christopher's Hospital in Brooklyn. Ocey Snead grew increasingly weak, almost wan, as though under the influence of a drug.

At one point, Virginia Wardlaw showed Dr. Pettit a will in which Ocey bequeathed most of her estate to her grandmother, reserving, however, one thousand dollars for his services. Dr. Pettit rejected the idea of a sum he considered greatly excessive and decided to report the entire matter to the police. He could not recall their making anything more than a routine inquiry, which led nowhere.

Dr. Pettit engaged a nurse after the operation and continued his calls. Far earlier than he wished, the women discharged the nurse. He himself was made to feel increasingly unwelcome. On his last visit no one answered the bell. Concerned with the welfare of his patient, in whose nature he sensed a quality of beauty, almost of spirituality, Dr. Pettit climbed into the house through a front window. He hurried to the invalid Ocey, whom he found in bed, nearly starved, with no food in the house. She greeted him with an eager smile and it seemed to him that she wanted to talk. At that moment one of the women in black came in and the invalid's smile vanished. Dr. Pettit ordered food to be sent for. Then, on request, he left.

"At no time was I able to find out from Mrs. Snead anything about herself," said the physician. "Every time I asked a question, one of the old women was always ready to give an answer. Mrs. Snead seemed afraid to talk. She appeared to me to be refined. What I could never understand was why such a woman would voluntarily live with such persons as her attendants. They looked disreputable to me. They were careless about their appearance and unfitted for association with refined people. But they never left her alone. I gave up the case because the elderly women did not take care of Mrs. Snead the way I wished. They refused to let me take the stitches out of the wound made in the operation on her. The stitches may be there now."

Dr. Pettit had reported the matter to the Brooklyn authorities. Since there was no tangible evidence of wrongdoing, they took no action. It was the doctor's belief that the interest he had aroused was the primary cause of the family's moving away.

Next on O'Neill's agenda was a visit to the nurse employed by Dr. Pettit, Miss Elizabeth Mogg of 273 East 39th Street, Flatbush. Miss Mogg had been called in to the case on August 18. On that day shortly before noon, Dr. Pettit performed his operation on Ocey Snead. The nurse stayed that afternoon and evening, leaving between midnight and one o'clock the following morning.

"Mrs. Snead did not want me to go," she recounted. "She wanted me to stay all night, but the other women, who never left us alone, insisted upon my leaving, saying they could take care of Mrs. Snead. I did not have any conversation with Mrs. Snead whatever. I could not because the other women did not give me a chance. Wherever I went one of them kept tagging after me. I was not alone with Mrs. Snead for a single moment. Mrs. Snead seemed afraid of someone or something. While I was near she clung to my hand and squeezed it. She seemed to want to tell me something but she did not dare to as one of the other women was present in the room all the time. About half an hour before midnight the front doorbell rang and one of the women went to the kitchen and yelled down the speaking tube. She told the caller to wait on the stoop a minute and went to a front room, taking care to close the hall door after her. I heard her raise the window and talk to someone. A man's voice answered. I am positive of that. The woman spoke in a slow, deliberate voice, and all she said was, 'Come later; someone here.'"

After this visit, Sergeant O'Neill placed two telephone calls. The first was to St. Christopher's Hospital at 283 Hicks Street, Brooklyn. An official told him David Pollock Snead had been brought to the hospital by a woman who said she was his aunt. At first this woman visited the baby regularly, promising to pay later for his care. Recently her visits had ceased. She had never paid. The baby, sick on arrival, was still in ill health.

The second call, to the Flatbush police station, brought Captain John Dulfer to the phone. He had investigated Dr. Pettit's complaint. "I did not believe I was justified in securing a search warrant," the captain explained. "When the old woman met me at the door I asked her to let me look around. I got in but she refused to allow me to go upstairs. The lower floor was barren of furniture. I told her the things I had heard. She smiled and said, 'Well, that is our business and nobody else's, and I cannot see why you should interfere.' I detailed detectives Corr and Elwood to watch the house, which they did until the family moved away. Nothing came to me in the form of charges."

With Dr. Pettit at his side, O'Neill returned to the House of Mystery, where two "mysteries" were quickly resolved. The spots on the floor, Dr. Pettit said, were not blood but tobacco stains, the work of some careless chewer of the weed. Next, the physician held a lighted candle close to the ominous remains in the kitchen range. While they were similar in form to the femur and skull of a young child, the odor, he stated firmly, could only come from an animal. The corrective information came too late for the *World*'s reporter. That excited journalist had left to file his story, which appeared in the paper's next edition, a gruesome account of a supposed "baby farm" — how else account for the large milk deliveries? — operated for criminal purposes. "Three old crones lived with sick woman in weird house and refused to give medicines and barred nurse's way — human bones and hair in kitchen stove," read the paper's leads. A good number of these figments were rapidly picked up by other metropolitan dailies.

O'Neill's last visit of the day was to William E. Fee, an attorney with offices at 631 Grand Avenue, Brooklyn. Fee explained that he lived on East Eleventh Street in Manhattan. A friend of his, Miss Louke, presided over a nearby day nursery attached to the People's Home Mission Church. Virginia Wardlaw was a frequent visitor to the nursery, where she had struck up an acquaintance with its director. One day she spoke of business at hand and asked for the name of a good attorney. Miss Louke recommended Fee.

On September 8, the lawyer and Miss Louke were asked to come to a Flatlands house to draw up and witness the signing of a will. The terms of the document were dictated by Virginia Wardlaw, and assented to in a very listless manner by Ocey Snead, who signed her name in silence.

When Fee asked if there was a previous will, he was shown an earlier document, dated August 7, 1909, and witnessed by a Reverend and Mrs. Charles Purdy. The reason for revising it so soon, the Wardlaw woman explained, was that it made no provision for Mrs. Snead's baby. Therefore, she had been told, it might be ruled invalid. The baby's removal to a hospital was described to Fee, and he was told that the infant's father was dead.

Moved by what seemed to him peculiarities in the case,

Fee had made a copy of the newly drawn will. O'Neill read with great interest the following terms:

I, Ocey Wardlaw Martin Snead, of County of Kings, Borough of Brooklyn, city of New York and state of New York, being of legal age and of sound and disposing mind, do make this my last will and testament. First, I direct that my funeral expenses and just debts be paid. Second, I give my infant son the sum of $500 (five hundred dollars). Third, I give and bequeath all of the remainder of my estate, both real and personal, of which I may die possessed at the time of my death, to my grandmother, Martha Eliza Wardlaw. Fourth, I appoint my grandmother, Martha Eliza Wardlaw, the executrix of my estate, without bonds or security of any kind. Fifth, I appoint my grandmother, Martha Eliza Wardlaw, the guardian of the person and estate of my infant son, to act without bonds and to have unrestricted powers. Sixth, in the event of the death of my infant son, I direct that all property he shall have derived from me, revert to my grandmother, Martha Eliza Wardlaw. In witness whereof I have to this, my last will and testament, consisting of two sheets of paper, subscribed my name this eighth day of September, 1909.

Ocey W. M. Snead

Thereafter, Virginia Wardlaw visited Fee's office several times, seeking financial advice. Ocey Snead, she told him, owned three pieces of real estate, in Virginia, Ohio, and Georgia, worth a total of sixteen thousand dollars. A letter was produced offering four thousand dollars for one of them. On another occasion, his visitor told Fee that Ocey's life was insured for twenty thousand dollars. She presented five different New York Life Insurance Company policies in proof. Considerable money had been borrowed on these policies, she said, and sought counsel as to how best to obtain more.

While Sergeant O'Neill made his way back to East Orange, local authorities were summing up the results of their own day's activities. Detective Harry Riker, searching the cellar at 89 North Fourteenth, made a series of important finds. One was a New York newspaper dated Sunday, November 28, the day Ocey Snead lay dead in the upstairs bedroom. Another was a bundle containing a mass of life insurance policies drawn on the life of the drowned Ocey, and naming her grandmother as beneficiary.

Perhaps most significant of all were some missing props. Nowhere in the house could Riker find either a pen or ink. And yet the suicide note was written in black ink. Where had it come from? Where had it gone? Furthermore, it appeared that there had been no fire in the kitchen stove for many weeks past. And there was no towel in the bathroom.

During much of the day, Chief Bell had continued his interrogation of Virginia Wardlaw. Laconic, quick-witted, she was an easy match for the chief. Bell called in Police Commissioner William Sharp, as well as East Orange's Mayor William Cardwell. The end result was the same, a verbal fencing match which ended in a draw. The woman in black steadfastly refused to speak of her family or background. When the mayor spoke of the alleged neglect of Ocey Snead, her temper flared.

"All that is untrue," she declared. "Do you think I would allow a relative, my own flesh and blood, to be neglected?"

"Why would you allow the sick girl to take a bath when there wasn't a towel in the house?"

"Well, I guess she might have dried herself on her petticoat," came the gently scoffing answer.

Again and again the officials asked her why the niece's death went unreported for twenty-four hours. "Now what's the use of discussing that phase of the question?" Virginia Wardlaw said dryly. "You are skeptical about everything I have told you and were I to go on and repeat what I have already told you, you would not believe me. Certainly I don't have to account for every minute of my time to you and I am not going to either. When do you think you'll discharge me?"

When late in the evening Sergeant O'Neill arrived with his account of wills, indicating a further strong interest in property rights, and when medical testimony showed apparent neglect, even deliberate mistreatment of the dead woman, Chief Bell made his decision. He preferred a charge of murder against his prisoner.

"There wasn't fourteen cents' worth of stuff there and there was no ink nor anything that could have been used as a substitute for it," he told the press in explaining his action. "There was a holder, but no pen. This certainly indicates that the note must have been written elsewhere. We know Mrs. Snead wasn't out of the Fourteenth Street house from the day she was taken there. Consequently, without pen and ink, she positively could not have written the note.

"Contrast the meager foodstuffs in the house with the breakfast Miss Wardlaw orders in jail. The old woman orders grapefruit and cereal and says she wants her coffee strong. Besides, she calls for cider, saying she is required to drink it because of its medicinal values. No fear of her starving, as I believe Mrs. Snead did.

"At first I believed Mrs. Snead attempted to take a bath, was discovered in the tub by her murderer, and held under water until drowned. I am now satisfied, after the careful examination of the Fourteenth Street house, that there was no fire in the stove the night the young woman died. Consequently, there could have been no hot water, and a woman in Mrs. Snead's condition would hardly have bathed in cold water. Therefore, there seems no doubt that Mrs. Snead was carried to the tub, thrown into the water, and drowned."

3

ON WEDNESDAY MORNING Virginia Wardlaw was taken from her cell in Newark. She was put into a closed carriage and driven to the City Hall in East Orange, there to be formally arraigned for murder. The press corps was in full attendance. Spectators crowded the council chamber, morbidly fascinated by newspaper reports of a diabolical murder plot and dark secrets of two houses. ARREST AUNT OF BATHTUB VICTIM: CHARGE WILL PLOT, read the New York *Herald's* headline. "Death," said the story, "was wooed by studied neglect, which, nature proving too slow, was reinforced by drowning. Never in the history of New Jersey criminal prosecution has a case exposed such cruelly perverted instincts." The New York *Daily Tribune* told of a beautiful young victim alone among keepers and constantly afraid, her life a profound enigma. "The woman," said the paper, "was held a prisoner by three slovenly creatures of middle age, and there was an unknown man who was wont to skulk into the building at the dead of night." "The people, their time, and their way of living were a deep and sinister mystery to all who lived in the neighborhood. The place was shunned as if it sheltered a pestilence," said the Newark *Evening News.* "That greed and desire to secure her property were the moving causes leading to Ocey Snead's death, and that she had undergone a period of privation and was suffering from malnutrition, that she was alive when placed in the bathtub, were all demonstrated yesterday. . . . Ghoulish greed for wealth possessed by the victim is, in the opinion of the police, at the bottom of the case."

Commissioner Sharp gave reporters his impressions of the prisoner. "I tried to question her but she bluntly told me that she saw no reason why she should answer my questions, that she would rely upon her own record in life for her defense," he related. "She was calm, cool, resourceful. She gave every evidence of her determination to make the police prove their case and not to aid them in the least. She betrays no emotion whatever, nor does she show any grief over her niece's death."

One of the most intriguing elements of the case was the appearance of the prisoner. No one had yet seen the face of Virginia Wardlaw, save in shadowy outline. During the long hours of interrogation she had pulled the folds of her black cape tightly about her and never lifted the veils which fell over her features. Frank Small, head keeper of the county jail, informed reporters that not even he had seen her. In her desolate cell, Virginia Wardlaw had completely isolated herself from view, placing wadded bits of newspaper in all the chinks which exposed her to the light. The matron, Mrs. John Schmidt, had visited the cell and seen her try to hide something under the folds of her clothes. She struggled briefly with her, and found a handbag with twenty-three dollars, a gold seal ring, and a wedding ring which she was told belonged to Ocey Snead. The matron confiscated the bag. Even during the struggle the veils had not lost their place.

All eyes were on Virginia Wardlaw when she entered the courtroom at ten o'clock with a detective on either side. Seeing the waiting crowd she drew back. A bailiff took her arm and led her up to the bar. Here she grasped the railing for support. She was dressed in the black cape-dress which she had worn throughout her two-day confinement. It came almost to the floor. The black mourning veil, of several thick-nesses, guarded her features. As Recorder Francis A. Nott, Jr., began speaking, she turned toward him.

"It is my duty to tell you that anything you say now may be used against you later," he said.

"Against?" she asked sharply. "I was told before that what I said might be used either for or against me."

"That is correct," the Essex County official acknowledged. "Remove your veil, madam."

"I do not wish to remove my veil."

"It is the order of this court that you remove your veil."

"You men would not like to see an old woman in tears."

"Please, madam, remove your veil."

"I must have a lawyer. My lawyer must see to this."

"Remove your veil so that you may be identified." Slowly, thoughtfully, Virginia Wardlaw raised her veils with both hands, bunching the cloth, pushing it upward until her face was partly revealed to the recorder. On each side, her palms remained outstretched so that those to the right and the left could see little. Only the recorder was permitted to gaze into a pair of discerning gray eyes fixed unwaveringly upon him, to see the wisps of dark gray hair straying out from under the veils, to note the high forehead, the aristocratic aquiline nose, and the firm closed mouth, before the veils dropped again.

Nott read Chief Bell's murder complaint, which accused the prisoner of "willfully and with malice aforethought caus-ing the death of Ocey W. M. Snead, whom she was sup-posedly nursing back to health." Death had been induced by drowning, said the charge; the object, profit which would eventually come to the defendant from certain insurance policies on the life of the deceased. The police chief asked that the prisoner be remanded to the county jail in Newark while he prepared his case for the grand jury.

As she heard the terrible charge, Virginia Wardlaw displayed no trace of emotion. Only as she was being led from the courtroom did she finally break down.

"I must have a lawyer," she suddenly exclaimed, her hitherto controlled voice choking as she went on. "I do not wish to see my poor niece buried in potter's field."

A chance visitor in the room was moved by the plea. Franklin W. Fort, son of the state's governor and a partner in the law firm of McLear and Fort, had come to the courthouse on business. Prompted by curiosity, he had stopped to see the arraignment of the woman in black. Now he offered to see that her request be granted. The court, recognizing him, allowed a brief conference with the prisoner. It was Fort who shielded her as she left the room, a thickness of newspaper under her veils to protect her from the photographers. Outside she entered a patrol wagon which took her back to Newark. There her handbag was returned to her.

"I do not believe persons not convicted of a crime should have their pictures taken against their wishes," Fort told the newspapermen. "I am not the counsel of this unfortunate woman. I have undertaken to see that her niece's body is given respectable burial and to communicate with her relatives in New York about it. I am not at liberty to give their names."

Later in the day, after a further visit with Virginia Wardlaw in her prison cell, the young lawyer said he had agreed to undertake her defense. He also registered a strong protest against the Essex County authorities. His client had written a letter and been allowed to give it to a messenger. Instead of letting him deliver it, however, police had taken possession of it themselves. Had the letter been intended for the post rather than hand delivery, the act of confiscation would have been a criminal offense, said Fort. As it was, the move was simply dishonorable.

4

THE WOMAN IN BLACK had found a defender. As the day wore on, it became obvious that she was sorely in need of one. Alerted by press accounts, new witnesses came forth with strange tales relating to the macabre "bathtub tragedy," as the case was increasingly referred to.

In East Orange, Mrs. Lydia Kane reported a bizarre encounter with Virginia Wardlaw. When her husband, engineer Henry Kane, obtained a job in Paterson, the Kanes had decided to move, advertising their Wakeman Avenue house for rent. Returning from a shopping trip, Mrs. Kane found a slip of paper under the door. A lead pencil scribble inquired about the terms of the rent and asked whether the house had a good-sized bathtub. The name Snead was signed to the note, while the address listed was 11 Clinton Street, Brooklyn. Two days later, at seven in the morning, Virginia Wardlaw appeared at the Kane residence, dressed in black, veils shrouding her face. She asked immediately whether the house had a large bathroom. On viewing it she said it was too small, then changed her mind and said she would rent the house. She wanted immediate occupancy. By now Mrs. Kane felt something "queer" in the air. She said she would have to ask her husband before committing herself. The visitor left and did not return.

A Flatlands neighbor of the House of Mystery, Mrs. Joseph W. Johnson, told police that before taking Ocey Snead's baby boy to the hospital, Virginia Wardlaw wanted a photo of him, but not from a professional photographer. She had asked Mrs. Johnson to bring her camera, which she did. She found the House of Mystery so dark that she was unable to get a picture. When asked to make a second attempt, Mrs. Johnson refused, unwilling to enter the gloomy premises a second time.

A professional photographer was evidently the next resort. Christian Martini, of 1546 Flatbush Avenue, provided the details: "On August 21 last, a woman wearing a black dress and a heavy black veil called at my store and asked whether I could go out to her house with my camera and take a picture of a sick woman in bed there. When I said that I could, she wrote on the back of one of my billheads: *No. 1693 East Forty Eight Street, 10:30 o'clock Sunday morning, August 22*. The writing was in lead pencil and in an irregular hand. On the date she requested I went to the house and was led to a room where a beautiful young woman was lying in bed with a child beside her. There were two old women in the room while I made the flashlight. The woman in bed appeared to be very weak and was propped up with difficulty. She paid me two dollars for my trouble in coming to the house. The woman, whom I believe to have been Miss Virginia Wardlaw, called at my store four days later. She said she would show the proofs to the sick woman and if they were satisfactory, she would get a large order. She said she wanted to send some of the pictures to the sick woman's husband in the South and other relatives of the sick woman. She bought a small hand camera before leaving the store. She came to my store again on November 20 and wanted to know if I would buy some films from her. I refused to buy them and have never seen her since that day. She did not, after taking the proofs, order any of the photographs."

Intrigued by the preoccupation with the size of the bathtub and by the possibility, suggested by Martini's statement, that Ocey Snead's husband was still alive in August, police authorities listened attentively as additional accounts came in. J. B. Hoecker, an optician at 312 Fulton Street, Brooklyn, said that in early fall Virginia Wardlaw asked permission to have her mail and telegrams addressed to his shop, leaving two dollars to pay for any wires that came in. When telegrams started pouring in, addressed to a J. H. Baskett, the deposit was quickly exhausted and further messages were returned to the telegraph office. One day a carriage drove up with the woman in black and a younger woman inside. Virginia Wardlaw referred to the latter as the J. H. Baskett of the correspondence. Hoecker informed the pair that they could no longer use his shop as a maildrop. Thomas H. Gardner, another Fulton Street optician, told a similar story.

A. E. Carroll, of 103 Montague Street, Brooklyn, a notary connected with a real estate company, said that Virginia Wardlaw came to his office on September 1, asking how much it would cost to have him acknowledge a loan on some life insurance policies. Carroll told her twenty-five cents. On the night of September 5 she came to his home, the address of which she had requested, and asked if he could come to a house in Flatlands to take some acknowledgments. Because the hour was late, Carroll refused. Two nights later she called again, with another, more slightly built woman in black and a young woman named Ocey Snead. This time acknowledgments were taken, all signed by Ocey Snead, and witnessed by Carroll. Several days later the women in black called still another time at Carroll's home, again at night, and asked him to witness still further signatures by Ocey Snead. Since the latter was not present, and Carroll had not seen the signatures made, he refused to give them his stamp. On each visit, Virginia Wardlaw had brought a bottle of ink and a pen with her, which the lawyer had remarked as peculiar at the time.

More financial troubles and a clue to the family's Southern background were provided by W. W. Butcher, a lawyer at

215 Montague Street, Brooklyn. On September 11, said Butcher, two women in black called on him, asking him to represent them against an insistent creditor in Virginia who held a mortgage on some pianos owned by the women and who was clamoring for money. Butcher recommended that they retain a lawyer on the scene. This was impossible, they told him, for their connections in the South were so close that almost everyone was related. They preferred a disinterested party as counsel. Money would be coming in soon from the death of a member of the family, they said. This would clear up all debts. They only wanted to stave off this man until then. Butcher obligingly drew up two pages of questions regarding the property. The women in black took them, paid him five dollars, and never came back.

The most graphic and telling recital came from Julius V. Carabba, another lawyer, located at 164 Montague Street, Brooklyn. "On September 9, a woman heavily veiled called at my office," Carabba began. "After some inquiries she asked me if I would like to invest a little money where I would get a return of one hundred dollars for every dollar I put in. Then she said that she wanted a will altered, the will of a dying woman, and that it must be done quickly. A previous document, drawn by a lawyer named Fee, she said, had not been properly witnessed. I told Miss Wardlaw — who would not tell me her name then, but I learned it later — I was willing to help her if the person making the will was of sound mind, and if everything else was in legal form. When I asked for the address, she refused to give it, saying she would have to look up my firm and that if everything was right she would call again the next day. Next day she called us up on the telephone and wanted my partner, Mr. Charles H. Schwartzmann, and myself to come up to number 1693 East 48th Street, Flatlands, that night. 'Don't ring the bell,' she said over the phone. 'I will be watching from the window, and don't make any noise as the people around here are very inquisitive.' She still would not give me the name of my prospective client."

It was a rainy night, Carabba said. He and his partner were apprehensive about the job, which looked too mysterious, but nonetheless they went to the designated house. From a distance they saw, at a downstairs window, the woman in black, who opened the door for them very quickly, then silently ushered them upstairs. The house was bare, with not even a chair for them to sit on. In the corner of one small room they saw a cot and lying on it a young woman who must once have been beautiful, with a magnificent head of auburn hair. Her face was sallow and emaciated, however, giving almost the appearance of a corpse.

Also in the room, seated on the edge of the cot, was a second elderly woman in black, whom Virginia Wardlaw introduced as her sister. She then sat down beside her, while the two lawyers, standing, contemplated the eerie scene. Both the elderly women wore hats and heavy veils. Round their necks were strung long strands of black beads, and in their hands were Bibles. From these they chanted at times, while making strange passes and motions toward the sick woman — Ocey Snead, as the lawyers found out. The latter lay watching the two as though in a coma, seemingly unable to move or to say a word. Suddenly, in a weird voice, one of the women asked her if she did not want to make out a new will. The passes going on all the time, the sick woman answered clearly, as if impelled by a strange power: "Yes, I do."

"My God, women, this woman is dying!" Carabba exclaimed. "She needs a doctor and nourishment and care. I'll get a doctor."

The outburst seemed to frighten the pair. No, the one said, they did not want a doctor, could not afford one, and in any event, the patient was dying. Carabba again said she needed food, but the old women said they had none, nor any money to buy some. The lawyer took out his checkbook, reflected a moment, then pretended he had no pen. As he hoped, the duo hurried downstairs to look for one. The minute the door closed behind them a remarkable change came over the woman on the cot. She mustered up a great effort and turned toward Carabba, who drew close.

"I'm dying," she whispered. "I'm dying. I see a Masonic pin on you and I believe I can trust you. Oh, for God's sake, please don't leave me. Here, here," she muttered feverishly, reaching under the pillow and dragging out a paper. "This is my will. Take it and make yourselves the executors. Do anything you like, but for God's sake take care of my child! Don't, please don't make that will like they will tell you to make it. Draw it so that my infant son and my grandmother will get my property. Also, please take me away from here. They are starving me to death and they will not give me any medicine."

Seeing that time was short, the dumbfounded lawyers hastily opened the will. It provided five hundred dollars for Ocey's infant son, and bequeathed all the rest of her estate to her grandmother, Martha Eliza Wardlaw. Conforming to Ocey Snead's instructions, they quickly scratched two changes into the document, the first saying that the son's five hundred dollars was "to be held in trust for him by Julius V. Carabba," and the second substituting Carabba's name for that of the grandmother as executor. The changes had barely been made, and the will thrust into Carabba's pocket, when the two old women returned. Carabba wrote out a check for five dollars but Ocey Snead now said she could not cash a check. As Carabba handed her a five dollar bill, he caught sight of two brand-new twenty dollar bills in a bag held by one of the women.

"Why, I thought you had no money!" he exclaimed.

"That is pension money and doesn't belong to us," said Virginia Wardlaw.

The latter, evidently the family spokesman, now disclosed the alterations she and her sister wished made in their niece's will. The grandmother, she said, was too old to be the beneficiary and executrix. Instead, the sisters should be named in a new document. If he would make the changes, she said, Carabba would receive two insurance policies on Ocey Snead's life, one for five thousand dollars, one for two thousand, both held by New York Life. There were other insurance policies, she said, with Metropolitan Life and Equitable, the whole totaling over twenty-four thousand dollars, and the ailing niece's estate would also include property in several Southern states with a value of over a hundred thousand dollars.

Refusing to deal with them unless they allowed him to bring in a doctor, Carabba was finally permitted to summon Dr. J. Wachsman from a nearby Flatbush office at 514 47th Street. Wachsman examined Ocey Snead and found nothing basically wrong with her except that she needed care and nourishment. He angrily upbraided the two sisters for their neglect of her, tossing the beads and Bibles they had left on the cot into a far corner of the room. He pushed back the curtain to let in the light. He gave instructions on proper treatment and asked to be informed next day of the patient's condition.

While Dr. Wachsman was making his examination, the two lawyers slipped downstairs to explore the house. They were sure they heard footsteps in the front room but found the door locked. Returning to the upstairs bedroom, they inquired about this. They were told an old nurse lived in the barred room. The sisters refused to show the lawyers any other part of the house.

At this point Carabba said that before making the required changes in Ocey Snead's will, he thought the consent of the grandmother should be obtained. To this the sisters objected strenuously. Carabba and his partner thereupon left the house, glad to be outside even though it was a dark night and raining. Dr. Wachsman left with them. The report he requested on the sick woman's condition was never rendered.

At his office, Dr. Wachsman confirmed essentials of the account Carabba had given to the police.

5

WHILE FOLLOWING THE MULTIPLICITY OF LEADS which were developing, sending detectives to several cities in both North and South, authorities gave priority to one key aspect of the case — the insurance on the life of Ocey Snead. A check with Equitable revealed three such policies, while the New York Life Insurance Company and Metropolitan Life together had records of four, the total value of all seven amounting to twenty-four thousand dollars. They had been taken out over a period of years, beginning in 1900, when Ocey Snead was only fifteen years old. Most of the policies were twenty-year endowments; some were thirty-year plans. At first they were payable annually; but later most of the premiums had been made payable quarterly, indicating financial strain. Furthermore, loans had been taken out on every one of the policies to the limit of their borrowing power.

At the offices of New York Life, officials were familiar with the account, one which had puzzled, intrigued, and also troubled them. The file was one of the liveliest in their memory. Policies were constantly being lost by the client, and duplicates issued. In several cases, the duplicates were lost and triplicates issued. This worried officials, who feared the multiple copies might well have served as bait for the obtaining of loans which had not been registered. Again and again, too, the policies were reassigned from one member of the family to another, again leading to a multiplicity of documentation which the company felt might be put to misuse.

In the course of these manipulations, Ocey Snead had often made her appearance at the New York Life offices, where she was remembered as kindly and beautiful. On almost every visit she was accompanied by her aunt, Virginia Wardlaw, who was the chief negotiator for the family. Superintendent J. H. Haskell of the policy claims department recalled the aunt with awe, and especially one of her last visits, on October 29, 1909. She had come to the office at 346 Broadway to see about the reassignment of one of the policies, asking so many complex questions that an amazed clerk reported the matter to Haskell. The latter asked the woman in black to put her questions in writing, since they might demand extensive analysis.

"She did not go home and write a letter," said Haskell, "but sat down and in a free, running hand wrote a series of questions which showed her familiarity with every phase of insurance. It was a remarkable document — so remarkable that a warning against her was spread upon the records of the company."

For the investigating detectives, Haskell produced the document, which read as follows:

How is the insured's endowment affected by the absolute assignment? How is the incontestability of the said policies affected by an absolute assignment?

How are the dividends under these policies affected by the absolute assignment? What is meant at this time by the phrase "subject to the conditions of the policy"?

What rules and regulations of the company are implied in the assignment blank? Does the company, or its officer, sign the duplicate of assignment returned to the insured?

Does this signed statement serve the insured as a receipt of the assignor?

Please explain what is meant by validity of assignment? Does the fact that the company has no responsibility for the validity of an assignment imply that an absolute assignment is open to any contest or otherwise? By whom could any contest be made in case of an absolute assignment made on the company's prescribed blanks and filed in the company's records?

In last paragraph of notice at foot of blank, please state if a New York City notary, with registered number and seal, must have his signature attested by the clerk of a court of record?

These highly subtle inquiries were penned as from "Ocey W. M. Snead, by Virginia O. Wardlaw."

Several phone calls elicited details of the extensive borrowing which had been done on the insurance policies. Louis Hartman, a notary connected with Iden and Company, at 42 University Place, Manhattan, was named in several documents. He told police that Virginia Wardlaw and her niece had come to his office in 1908 with a sad tale of financial troubles. To him they seemed to be cultivated people fallen on bad times. He became interested in them and made them a loan of six hundred twenty dollars. As security, they gave him certain deeds on Southern property. Later they asked him to return the deeds and in exchange he accepted a claim against an insurance policy on the life of Ocey Snead.

Dr. M. S. Gabriel, of 412 West 23rd Street, Manhattan, was named in another document. He recalled the visit of several women in black, who asked him to attend a young girl for tonsillitis. Instead of paying for his services, they showed him three insurance policies, the money on which they expected to realize shortly. "You see, we're good for your fee," one of them had said. He nonetheless asked for a written confirmation of the loan, which they gave him.

In banks around the city, detectives found insurance policies on the life of Ocey Snead deposited as security for loans. Some were registered with the issuing companies, some not. The network of loans was immensely complex and ingenious, stretching out in every conceivable direction for funds. From William Cummings, an officer of New York Life, came a tribute to the engineer of these transactions. "With all my wide knowledge of life insurance in every branch, I doubt if I am as familiar with methods, figures, and business in general as was the person whose handwriting appears on the mass of papers we've examined," said Cummings. "It is not remarkable, but astounding!"

One of New York's police commissioners, Elijah S. Boettler, gave the findings a somewhat different interpretation. "I believe these women have been working insurance company swindles for ten or twelve years," he declared.

As detectives followed up each clue, the picture that emerged was of a carefully reared structure of insurance policy loans, hypothecations, and lapsed premiums near collapse. By adroit manipulation, seven policies with a value of more than twenty-four thousand dollars had been maintained over a period of years. By November 1909, however, the policies had been drained of all potential; they could yield no more except by the death of Ocey Snead. In that event, all sums would go to Martha Eliza Wardlaw, the grandmother, whom the records showed to be eighty-four years old and nearly blind. Upon Ocey's death, only the slender thread of life in this feeble old woman would keep the proceeds from falling into the hands of the sisters in black.

Each bit of information on the case was turned over, as it came in, to Wilbur A. Mott, the public prosecutor for Essex County. After slightly more than two days of investigation, Mott made a statement: "The facts as they are developing point more and more surely to the conclusion that Mrs. Snead's death was the result of foul play. No effort or expense will be spared to develop all the clues in our possession."

6

THE POLICE WERE SATISFIED that Virginia Wardlaw was the aunt of Ocey Snead, that Ocey's husband Fletcher was perhaps still living, that their child was in a Brooklyn hospital. They knew that Virginia Wardlaw had two sisters who also habitually dressed in black, and that an aged grandmother figured in the case. Where were the other sisters, however, and the grandmother? And where, if alive, was Fletcher Snead? And what was the explanation for the contrast between the family's obvious culture, the clear evidence of an upper stratum of society, and its present dire poverty? Why did Virginia Wardlaw refuse to clear up these puzzling questions?

By Thursday, December 2, answers began to pile in, overwhelming in their abundance, startling and contradictory in content. Neighbors of the House of Mystery had said the family stored its belongings with Eagle Warehouse and Storage at 28 Fulton Street, Brooklyn. A search through their files revealed nothing under the name of either Wardlaw or Snead. Then detectives remembered that Ocey Snead's baby was named David Pollock. Thinking Pollock might be another branch of the family, authorities made a second search. It was successful. Under Pollock they found a sizable quantity of furniture, handsome pieces in good repair, along with a dozen trunks containing clothing, family records and other documents, and countless bundles of newspaper clippings.

They had only begun to sift through the masses of material when another rich cache presented itself. Dr. F. O. Collins, proprietor of a drugstore at 131 Third Avenue, Manhattan, contacted the police. Late one night in May, he stated, a heavy-set woman dressed all in black entered his store, asking permission to leave a large package of papers for safekeeping. The next day the woman reappeared with another large bundle, insisting they be held for her personally, no matter who called, or on what pretext. Collins thought this strange, but acceded to her request. After three days, another elderly woman, dressed in black and heavily veiled, called at the drugstore. She said the first caller, her sister, was ill, and that she needed the papers. Collins refused to turn them over, much to the woman's displeasure. Neither caller ever returned. The second, Collins said, corresponded to the published description of Virginia Wardlaw. At a later date, Collins said, still another package had been left by a well-dressed young man whom he now suspected of being Fletcher Snead. New York police were beginning to examine the various contents, all still tied in bundles, when East Orange authorities joined them.

To their amazement, the assembled detectives found they were dealing with one of the great families of the South, a branch of the old and respected Wardlaw clan. From bits and pieces of documentation scattered through suitcases and packages, and aided by quick references to an encyclopedia, the picture began to round itself out. It revealed connections in Georgia, Virginia, Kentucky, and Tennessee. Ties were found to the McGowans, the Perrins, the Moormans, the Lewises, the Parkers, the Witherspoons, and other old families that shaped the life of the South in antebellum days.

John Baptist Wardlaw, born in Georgia in 1816, was one of a family of twelve children. He had married Martha Eliza Goodal, an Easterner, and become one of the most prominent Methodist clergymen of his time, a scholarly man, greatly respected. Six children came from the union: Caroline, Mary, Virginia, John, Albert, and Bessie. John Baptist had died in 1896, but his wife Martha Eliza was the grandmother whose whereabouts police were trying to ascertain in New York.

Of the offspring, records showed that the eldest, Caroline, was born in 1845, making her present age 64. She had married Colonel Robert M. Martin of Louisville, Kentucky. Their child was named Ocey. Mary, three years younger than Caroline, had married a Confederate veteran and prominent lawyer named Fletcher T. Snead. Well-known in Georgia, Snead was several times mayor of the city of Oglethorpe, and also held county offices. To the couple were born three children, boys named Fletcher, John, and Albert. Records showed that Ocey Martin had married young Fletcher Snead, her first cousin.

Virginia Wardlaw, born in 1852, had remained single. She was now fifty-seven. John had died in 1881 at the early age of twenty-seven. Albert was apparently living in the South, as was Bessie, a much younger late addition to the family.

Indications were that Caroline Martin, Mary Snead, and Virginia Wardlaw were all in the New York area, although only the latter's whereabouts, in the Newark jail, were definitely known.

Reaching into the past, John Baptist Wardlaw's father was William Wardlaw, reputed as a great hunter. His father, in turn, was Hugh Wardlaw, a captain who fought against the British during the Revolutionary War. Hugh's father was named William Wardlaw, born in 1700 in Scotland. It was William's father, Robert Wardlaw, born near Glasgow, Scotland, in 1670, who decided to make the move to America, settling in Pennsylvania around 1720 and twenty years later moving on to Virginia.

In the South, the Wardlaw family could boast of a distinguished array of church divines, merchants, lawyers, bankers, surgeons, and public officials. Among them were David Lewis Wardlaw, one of the most eminent judges of his day, a Speaker of the House of Representatives of South Carolina, later an Associate Justice of the Court of Appeals; and Francis Hugh Wardlaw, a famous jurist who prepared the original draft of the Ordinance of Secession and whose legal opinions were models of rhetorical beauty.

Even more impressive were more distant family antecedents abroad.

The Wardlaws were said to have come to England from Saxony early in the sixth century. They were among the original Anglo-Saxon refugees who at the time of the Norman Conquest fled and escaped into Scotland. The name Wardlaw was mentioned in the records of Hexham, in England, as early as 883, when Alfred the Great was king; and in Scotland it appeared in a document in 1210, when a parish of that name was cited in Inverness-shire. By the latter half of the thirteenth century the surname began to be used. In 1630 a Scottish baronetcy was created for Sir Henry Wardlaw, 1st Knight Baronet of Balmule and Baron of Petreavie, County Fife, with a coat of arms showing a shield or field of blue, three lozenges of gold, three water bougets of gold, and the crest of a golden star. The motto was *Familias firmat pietas.* In the eighteenth century many Scottish families, including the Wardlaws, migrated to the United States, drawn by the promise of religious freedom.

The two most distinguished Scottish representatives of the clan were Bishop Henry Wardlaw, founder of St. Andrew's University, the earliest in Scotland, and Walter Wardlaw. For nearly a century these two men figured prominently in the history of their country and of England and Europe. In 1383 Pope Clement VII made Walter a cardinal, the first Scottish churchman ever so named. A third divine, Congregationalist Ralph Wardlaw, a nineteenth-century antislavery crusader, was responsible for inviting Harriet Beecher Stowe to visit Scotland in 1853.

One other family ancestor deserves to be mentioned, Lady Elizabeth Wardlaw, who in 1719 published the ballad of "Hardyknute" and circulated it as a fragment of an ancient poem. She had discovered the work, she said, in a vault in Dunfermline, but when no original manuscript was forthcoming skeptics began to doubt her word. Several of her friends, professing to be intimately acquainted with the circumstances of its production, positively ascribed its authorship to her. The work had merit, all agreed, but was it genuine, truly an ancient poem? Or was it a skillful literary forgery?

7

IN HER CELL, Virginia Wardlaw gave a long sigh when confronted with the family background, but refused to break her silence, declined to give the precise present location of the family in the South, or to cite the name of a single friend who might come to her aid. She was innocent, she insisted; her treatment at the hands of police an outrage. Authorities asked themselves if this haughty self-possessed woman, born to a proud name, could conceivably be the murderer of her own niece.

Unable to gain information from the principal in the case, they searched the trunks and bundles they had found for clues which might be helpful. Rent bills and receipts sent detectives to a dozen addresses in New York and Brooklyn, at each of which various members of the family had resided in the past two years. They showed a steady decline of position. The oldest recorded stays in fashionable East Side neighborhoods and expensive hotels, including the Brevoort, the Chelsea, and the Waldorf-Astoria. These gave way to more moderate accommodations and finally to the threadbare existence in the twin Houses of Mystery in Brooklyn and East Orange.

Often the later rent bills were unpaid, the tenants forced to move by the landlord. Each move entailed the delivery of trunks stuffed with documents, including voluminous clippings from newspapers of cities all over the country. Detective O'Neill noted that these often fell into a pattern, many dealing with narrow escapes from death or death from violence under peculiar circumstances. One, for example, told of a party drifting out to sea in an open boat, of the harrowing period of danger, and the eventual rescue. Another told of a woman killed in an automobile accident soon after a miraculous recovery from illness.

Among the bills, the one with the latest date bore a Manhattan address, 466 West 22nd Street. That number was at the same time given to authorities by Henry Hegeman of 493 West 22nd. Hegeman said a woman in black had employed him as a stenographer but refused to pay the bill. Detectives O'Neill and Riker hurried to the spot. Their call was abundantly rewarded. From Mrs. Cathleen Bond, the housekeeper, they learned that three women in black, the redoubtable sisters, as well as Ocey Snead and the aged grandmother, had all resided there until recently. Even now, Mrs. Mary Snead and the grandmother were living in the house!

"They were the queerest I ever saw," said Mrs. Bond. "They kept their doors and windows closed all the time and the lights on until we had to turn the gas off for fear they would do some harm. They would not let us into the room even to clean it up. The one who called herself Mrs. Morton or Mrs. Martin, but who was called Mrs. Maxwell by the 'aged,' as they spoke of the oldest one of the crowd, was the first to appear. She gave me fifty cents to allow mail to be delivered to her here under various names. The others came shortly after. They got their own meals and had nothing to do with any of us. They said they were in the real estate business and had important papers which they did not want disturbed. There was one little black box which Mrs. Martin never let out of her sight. One day she said she did not have any money for the rent but the 'aged' was to get seven hundred dollars soon from Virginia, where she had property. Mrs. Martin left, saying she was going to look after the property. We were glad to see her go for she was the worst tempered of the lot. There was one we used to call 'the tramp' because she was all the time going in and out with a suitcase, running errands and doing the business for the others. This was Miss Wardlaw, a tall gaunt woman."

Mrs. Bond recalled that when the weird ménage arrived, all five women lived in an upstairs room from which they rigidly excluded even Mrs. Catherine Anderson, the landlady. The latter had tried to collect the rent but without success. It was when Mrs. Anderson objected to so many women in one room that Mrs. Martin had left on her journey and Virginia Wardlaw and Ocey had gone to East Orange. The grandmother and Mary Snead had changed to a cheaper room in the basement.

After they had moved out, Mrs. Martin and Miss Wardlaw sometimes came back to visit, said Mrs. Bond. On Monday last, the day on which Ocey Snead proved to have been lying dead in East Orange, the grandmother and her daughter, for some unexplained reason, suddenly pulled down the blinds, locked the doors, and kept the gas burning all day until ordered to put it out.

In the basement quarters, detectives and reporters found Mary Snead, a gentle, soft-spoken woman dressed in the same black garb worn by her sister Virginia, veils shielding her face from full view. Her figure was slighter, more delicate than Virginia's. Iron-gray hair, worn in an old-fashioned style, was fixed in small curls flattened against the temples. What could be seen of the features showed them to be comely. The aged grandmother was huddled in a corner, in a weak condition, almost blind from cataracts. The room was sparsely furnished. There was no food in sight, little sign that the quarters had actually been lived in.

When told Virginia Wardlaw had been charged with the murder of Ocey Snead, the two women displayed little emotion, receiving the news stoically, as silent as Virginia herself. Again and again, like her, they refused to answer questions. Finally a detective persuasively suggested that speaking out might help their relative, who was after all in the most trying circumstances, charged with the most serious of crimes.

"Miss Wardlaw was the kindest of women to our little girl!" Mary Snead at last burst out, her voice anguished as she spoke of the dead. "She was delicately nurtured and guarded with the most tender care. Miss Wardlaw never harmed a hair of our little girl's head. We have been cruelly treated. Our private affairs have been inquired into. It is terrible."

The sudden effort at speech was upsetting. The two detectives waited while Mary Snead made an effort to control herself. After a moment she continued, her manner thoughtful, her voice soft but clear.

"In the hope of lightening the burden of an innocent woman I will tell all I know," she said. "There is no mystery in the case. There was no mystery in our living in the modest Flatlands house. There is nothing to conceal except for the sake of our family and relatives and it was for them that we have been silent until now."

"My daughter-in-law, the poor girl who died in the East Orange house, before her marriage was Ocey Wardlaw Martin. She was born in this city twenty-four years ago, the daughter of the late Colonel Robert Martin, a gallant Confederate officer. Soon after the war Colonel Martin — that was his army rank — came to New York to enter the merchandise house of David Dows. I am not sure that that firm even exists now. Indeed I don't think it does, as this was many a year ago, and Colonel Martin himself has been dead many years. He was the tobacco inspector for the house, judging the quality of all the tobacco which the house exported to its European customers. Colonel Martin was a

man of high education and received a large salary for his
services. The family lived in ease and comfort in one of the
most desirable residential sections of New York in those
days.

"Ocey and my son, Fletcher W. Snead, who I am sure is
dead, were own cousins, I being the sister of the mother.
Ocey and my son, therefore, had known each other from
childhood up. He used to come to New York from his home
in the South to visit the home of his aunt, and Ocey almost
every year came south to my home for long visits. When she
grew up, her father was anxious for her to be educated in
the South and, although living in the North, to grow up as a
Southern girl. For that reason he sent her to school near our
old home in the South. Though my son and she did not go to
the same school they were educated not far from each other
and were frequently together. From being friends they became sweethearts and were married in the South in 1906.
About a year later they came to New York, going to live at
28 East Eleventh Street. Here the first child was born. It
died two days after its birth.

"My daughter-in-law had some money, some property in
the South, which had come to her from her father, and years
before she was married her life had been insured for the
benefit of her estate. My son roamed around a good deal
after his college days. He finally got employment in a lum-
beryard here in the summer of 1908, remaining there until
early in the present year, when he was discharged. Some
months later he decided to go south for his health. We have
never seen him since. Soon after his departure a message
came to his wife that he was dead. We have no reason to
doubt the truth of this report of his death.

"At the time my son went away my sister, Miss Virginia
Wardlaw, now held in East Orange, my daughter-in-law,
and myself were living in the house at 1693 East 48th Street,

Flatbush. We had gone there because we wanted quiet for my daughter-in-law, who was soon to become a mother a second time. She had been in ill health since the birth of the first child and was exceedingly nervous. We wanted to get away from the noise, from piano playing next door, and so selected this sparsely settled neighborhood. I rented the East Orange cottage and took Ocey there.

"I see a great mystery has been made of the fact that we rented both floors of the two-family house. There was no mystery. The rent for the two was only twenty-five dollars a month, and we got rid of the noise of a family above us. I see also that the neighbors are said to have been greatly alarmed because we lived in seclusion. We did live in seclusion. I say it in no disrespect to them that most of those in that section are of the working class, not particularly well educated, and we did not think we would find it congenial to mingle with them.

"Mrs. Martha Eliza Wardlaw, my mother and the grandmother of the dead girl, was never in that house. She lives here now but was then boarding in this city. She has lived here many years. The mother of Ocey Snead is not here. I will not say that she is dead. I will not say where she is. The fact is, I don't know. Probably she hasn't read of the death in the newspapers and so doesn't know about it. She was a teacher in the public schools in this city for thirty-three years and now enjoys a pension of a thousand dollars a year.

"All during the time we were in the Flatbush house my daughter-in-law was ill and despondent. She thought she was going to die, and of her own accord asked that a lawyer be obtained so she could make her will. She felt grateful to her grandmother for watching over her when she was a child, in the absence of her mother, and it was for that reason that she made her the beneficiary. She was not coerced in any way, and it is really silly to talk about our having power over her or hypnotizing her. She was not starved or mistreated. If she did not get any fresh meat, it was because she had what we had. We lived in the way we did for convenience.

"After the birth of the child it had been put in a home. We came to Manhattan to look for a place to spend the winter. Miss Wardlaw went out to East Orange and she and my daughter-in-law were to see how they liked it there before my mother and I went out. If they liked it we were to take out our furniture, now in storage. Then the poor girl, ill in body and mind, ended it all, and this terrible charge was made against an innocent woman. Sometimes I sit here, fearing to show my face in the street and thinking what our people in the South will say if they hear of it. I nearly go crazy. I never even heard of Ocey's death until I saw it in the papers this morning."

After this long interview, Detectives O'Neill and Riker asked Mary Snead and her mother to come voluntarily to East Orange. The two women, frightened, would not leave their drab cell-like room. Since no crime had been committed in New York, the detectives had no alternative but to leave; however, they placed the house under surveillance of New York police.

8

ON THE SAME DAY, Thursday, December 2, lawyer Franklin Fort held conferences, first with Virginia Wardlaw and later with the two women at West 22nd Street. They were unexpectedly fruitful, leading Fort to make a statement which showed he believed strongly in the innocence of all concerned, especially Virginia Wardlaw.

"It is useless and impossible to attempt to deny specifically the articles which have been found in the newspapers on this very unfortunate affair," the statement read. "In the mass of partial truth and partial invention which has been published, however, weight seems to have been lost of one or two important facts. First, the only evidence yet produced as to the manner of Ocey Snead's death is in absolute accord with the story told by Miss Wardlaw. Death resulted from drowning. It is utterly inconceivable that drowning could have occurred in one foot of water without the assent, certainly, of the person drowned. Second, the insurance policies, to secure which, it is alleged, Ocey Snead was killed, are of comparatively long standing, the most recent being six years old. Every last one of them is an endowment policy. Nearly all of them had run for half their terms already, having been taken out, for the most part, nine years ago. Not a single policy is of the kind usually termed a straight life insurance policy, which is payable only on the death of the person taking it out. On all of these policies, loans had been taken out. It was the payment of more than a year and a half's interest on these loans, made on November 23, which accounted for the crippled condition of the family finances."

It was the bitter struggle to make ends meet, said Fort, that lay at the root of the clan's troubles. Every penny had been used to keep up the insurance premiums, the only security left in a welter of business losses, of declining fortunes. These policies were taken out at the insistence of the aunts, the mother, and the grandmother, all of whom had been teachers, and all of whom had met financial reverses. They were training Ocey Snead to be a teacher, too, and meant to protect her old age from the troubles which had beset their own. It was no doubt true that Ocey's stomach, at death, was empty, that she had been starving. But so were all the rest of the family. For more than a week, Fort said,

Mary Snead and her mother had been living on loaves of bread, until he had forced help upon them.

"They had expected remittances from Christiansburg, Virginia," continued the lawyer. "A school there which they had conducted was closed last January because of its financial failure, but out of the wreckage there was still something coming to the Wardlaws. Affairs had not been settled yet, however, and the remittances which they expected failed them therefore; with this money they had expected to get the furniture which is stored in New York. Had it come to hand the house would not have been unfurnished and they would have had temporary relief, at least, from the poverty which oppressed them.

"Miss Wardlaw's sole crime has been the possession of an intense pride," he concluded. "Pride of family and dread that their financial needs might get out has prevented her from speaking freely even to me, and in this matter of pride she differs no whit from the rest of her family. Theirs has been one long struggle, not only against poverty but against that poverty becoming publicly known. The lengths to which they went to keep this secret explains many things about their way of living. Miss Wardlaw would rather go to the electric chair than humble her pride by giving out details of family history that might appear discreditable in newspapers."

To show the character of his client, Fort released two of her letters, dated April 1908, which had come into his possession. They were sent from Christiansburg, Virginia, where she was then teaching, and where Ocey Snead had come to visit with her after the death, a short time before, of her first child. The letters were addressed to *My Darling Fettie*, the aunt's nickname for Fletcher Snead, who had remained at his work in New York. They were signed with the French word for aunt.

My Darling Fettie —

What a floodtide of loving sympathy flows to you this beautiful Sabbath afternoon, which is radiant with sunshine and cheerful with song birds, butterflies and blossoming trees! I wish you could sit by me in the perfect quiet and enjoy the restful stillness, the nerve-soothing beauty and calmness.

Precious darling, my heart aches to comfort and help you. I would love to hold your dear head on my lap and run my fingers through your hair and so charm away brain worry or heartache or tired spirit. May this little word of tenderness help you to understand that your mother's sister is your own loving "Tante," true to you, dear heart, and longing to put some joy and sweetness into your life.

May fortune or fate — or, better still, the Providence before us — give us the satisfaction of being together and proving in a daily companionship the fidelity and loyalty of our hearts to each other. Keep my place in your love ever open and warm and love me always.

I have no news. My love to all the others.

Faithfully,
Tante

My Darling Fettie —

I send this line of deepest sympathy in your grief over the loss of dear little Mary Alberta. Ah, precious child, you have had a full cup of sorrow, but your brave heart bears up under it all. I would gladly comfort you for the little one's death, but grief like that is healed only by the dear Father of us all.

On Easter Sunday dear little Ocey and I took purple lilacs to the dear graves in this cemetery, and in memory of the resurrection of Christ and the hope of the resurrection of our dead laid the symbols of life renewed on each of the pre-

cious mounds. I wish you could have been with us and I hope that some day little Mary Alberta will sleep there with our other precious dead. That you have a dear child in heaven is a holy thought that will, I trust, draw your heart and soul ever upward and lift you toward God and all sacred things. Be assured your Tante *ponders much over your life, your responsibilities and all the changes which have come to you. Stand fast, dear heart. Be true and faithful to your dear mother, your devoted grandmother, all the links of family life. I hope your next change will be to come to me and bring with you the others. Remember that they have suffered also and suffered, too, for you and with you in every grief that has come into your life, and give them whatever cheer, thoughtful attention, unselfish care for them, and sunny words may bring to their bruised hearts.*

Faithfully,
TANTE

It was inconceivable, said Fort, that the woman who wrote these compassionate letters, expressing such unreserved love for Ocey and Fletcher Snead, could later have murdered her niece by the gruesome act of drowning her in a bathtub. Soon, he said, he expected further evidence which would prove her innocence and lead to the dropping of all charges against her.

As if in confirmation of his views the lawyer at this time received a distinguished visitor. To his office came Dr. E. D. Lyons of Grandview, New York, a member of the class of 1877 at Princeton. One of the rarest privileges of his years at that institution, said Dr. Lyons, was his friendship with John Banks Wardlaw, the brother of the accused Virginia. Reading of the case in the papers, he felt compelled to offer his views.

John Wardlaw, he recalled, was one of the most brilliant scholars Princeton had ever turned out, known and loved by all. His friends included many men who later enjoyed great success in business or the professions; people like John A. Campbell, Walter Hines Page, Moses T. Pyne, George Armour, and Henry Fairfield Osborn. He had excelled in literature, receiving the Literary Fellowship at the school in 1878. On graduating, offers of teaching positions came from a dozen colleges in the East. John Wardlaw declined these flattering overtures to take a professorship in a Southern university. In 1880, at the age of twenty-six, he married Lizzie Davidson of Baltimore, only to have her die tragically a short time later. In 1881 his own promising career as a writer and educator was cut short by death.

"I know Miss Wardlaw and her sisters personally and there are no more refined and educated and cultured women in the country than they. I assure you she was one of the most brilliant women educators in the United States," Lyons said emphatically. "The Wardlaws came from a fine old Southern family. They had money in those days. I presume the family gradually lost money. There is not a word of truth in the press accusations against Miss Wardlaw. She and her sisters would never resort to a crooked transaction. The whole trouble is caused by the reticence of the aged women through family pride. The sisters were too proud to apprise friends of their poverty."

A terrible injustice was being perpetrated, Lyons said. He was ready to give of his own money and he also planned to visit the Princeton Club to ask other friends of John Wardlaw to help the family. "It is a duty which Princeton men of every class should meet manfully," he concluded. "I am happy to say that the time has arrived when Miss Wardlaw and her sisters can feel they are not alone in the world and without friends."

Bringing what he considered good news to Virginia Ward-law, Fort was dismayed to see that proud woman's reaction. "Has it come out that I am a sister of John's!" she lamented. "Oh, this is too terrible. Aside from Ocey's death this is the most awful blow my poor sisters and I myself have been dealt. He was such a magnificent man, such a brilliant mind, whose life was the noblest of any in the world, that it almost drives me crazy to think his name has been dragged into this case. It is beautiful of John's friends to have trust in us, but please don't have them give us financial assistance. Up to now I have had no one but you, Mr. Fort, and I am perfectly content to fight the battle with you."

Fort outlined the necessity for such assistance to his distraught client. After long resisting arguments, Virginia Wardlaw reluctantly agreed, and as a signal that the interview was over, withdrew to the far corner of the cell. There she sat on a backless chair, her eyes firmly closed, as though trying to shut out the inhospitable present.

9

ONE OF FORT'S FIRST ACTS the next day was to pay overdue rent on the room at 466 West 22nd Street, where Mrs. Anderson had threatened to evict her two elderly tenants. Thereafter, the fund raised by Princeton men provided a weekly allowance of twenty-five dollars to maintain them. Seeing that the aged grandmother was extremely weak and despondent, Fort made arrangements to transfer her to a suburban home where family friends could provide proper care. The lawyer than began gathering additional support for his contention that Virginia Wardlaw was innocent of the murder of her niece.

The authorities, meanwhile, were coming up with strong material of their own. In East Orange, twelve-year-old Charles Kirk remembered an encounter with a woman in black on Monday, November 29, the day that Virginia Wardlaw reported Ocey's death. Shortly after four in the afternoon, he saw the woman leaving her house, carrying a rope-bound satchel. She offered the young boy first five cents, then ten, then fifteen if he would carry the bag. Because her appearance frightened him, he refused. He watched as she herself carried her burden and mounted a streetcar bound for Newark.

Detective David Wendel located George Handschuh, the conductor of the car in question. He remembered the mysterious woman who rode with him that afternoon. She had alighted, he said, at High Street in Newark, just behind the county courthouse.

Within the hour, the woman in black was apparently back in East Orange. A witness was found who saw her return, seemingly deep in thought. This witness was intrigued by her bizarre dress and watched as she walked some five or six blocks past 89 North Fourteenth. Suddenly she straightened up and hurried back to the house. The bag was gone.

While removing all contents of the East Orange house where Ocey Snead died, police found something they had overlooked earlier. Far back on a closet shelf they came upon a pint bottle of whiskey, still half full. The brand name was one sold at Saat's Hotel, at Main and North Fifteenth, only a stone's throw from number 89. From the hotel bartender, Detective Wendel learned that a woman in black, answering to the description of Virginia Wardlaw, purchased the bottle at eight o'clock on Thanksgiving eve, November 24. Entering by a side door, she had asked for a pint of whiskey. She was about to leave when she noted a Negro standing at the bar. She asked the bartender to send him over. After a moment's discussion the two left together. The Negro returned two hours later, a broad smile on his face. When the bartender asked what the woman in black wanted, he said, "Oh, she wanted to convert me to her religion or something like that. I don't know just what." The Negro had hung around for an hour, ordering frequent drinks, before leaving the bar, where he was never seen again.

From the Negro colony in East Orange, Wendel learned that the man was a stranger in town, thought to be from New York. From neighbors of the Fourteenth Street house, he learned that a stocky Negro resembling the man at the bar had several times been seen loitering on the sidewalk late at night, gazing up at the windows of 89 North Fourteenth. One neighbor saw what she thought was this same Negro hovering in front of the house on the Sunday night of Ocey Snead's death. Usually the house was dark except for a light in the front room occupied by Ocey, but on this night the whole second floor was brightly lit, this person noted. Flitting before the curtained window, shadows of two persons were seen, those of a man and a woman.

"We are working on the theory that this black man carried the girl to the tub on instructions from Miss Wardlaw," Wendel told reporters. "We believe he was the man she met in the bar, and that after leaving the car in Newark she gave him her satchel to dispose of."

Bundles, satchels, suitcases full of material left by the three sisters were everywhere, it seemed, in restaurants and drugstores, stationery stores and delicatessens, in optical shops and telegraph offices, and of course at private residences. During the six weeks prior to vacating the Flatlands house in Brooklyn, the family had actually lived there very little, only stopping by to pick up needed items. Fearing eviction, they had sought to establish themselves elsewhere, in the process living at a dozen different addresses. This pattern apparently prevailed to some degree over the entire eighteen-month residency in Flatbush. Seemingly a loner, Mrs. Martin had frequently taken hotel rooms by herself. The grandmother was usually put up in a boardinghouse where she stayed until the nonpayment of the rent bill forced her to another lodging. Ocey Snead often stayed with her aunts, Virginia and Mary, at 11 Clinton Street, at 146 Henry Street, and at 977 Flatbush Avenue in Brooklyn; and in as many Manhattan dwellings, at first, good addresses at 261 East 28th Street and 28 East Eleventh Street, and later in poorer areas. For a time in the past spring she stayed with her grandmother at the Federation Hotel for Working Girls at 462 West 22nd Street, next door to the current domicile of Mary Snead. Later the grandmother was placed in a room at 468 West 22nd Street. Always the various relatives visited back and forth, strange black birds in hurried anxious flight who left behind documentary droppings.

Police searching this ever proliferating mass of material discovered more and more insurance papers, policies assigned and reassigned, many additional rough drafts of wills made out by Ocey Snead, all unsigned, including one which described a seventeen-acre plot of real estate in the South; also family photographs, letters received and letters written but never sent, endless files of newspaper clippings, and perhaps most important of all, ever increasing evidence of poverty, of dire financial straits. For police, this last condition was, of course, the motive they hoped to establish as having led to the murder of Ocey Snead. Money, the need for money, seemed indeed to be the overwhelming preoccupation of the three sisters. A new set of witnesses testified to its paramountcy. And where early accounts directed attention primarily to Virginia Wardlaw, the fresh wave seemed also to implicate Caroline Martin and, to a lesser extent, Mary

Snead, who had admitted to renting the East Orange house where Ocey's death had occurred.

At still another address, 412 East 23rd Street, Manhattan, the landlady reported the strange story of Eliza Enochs, the young sister of a wealthy Southern lumberman. Miss Enochs had stayed briefly at her boardinghouse, shepherded by the weird women in black who descended in separate waves. First to arrive was the stout Mrs. Martin. "My servants and maids are getting a house in readiness in Brooklyn for us, and perhaps we may be compelled to stay here some little time," she said grandly. Soon she was joined by Ocey Snead, a little later by Mary Snead and Virginia Wardlaw, and finally by the grandmother.

With Miss Enochs, all these women lived in one room. After the rent was six or seven weeks in arrears, the landlady discovered their poverty and asked them to leave. Thereupon the rent money was produced. The landlady learned, however, that they had borrowed six hundred dollars from Eliza Enochs, in exchange transferring to her, as beneficiary, an insurance policy on Ocey Snead's life with the proviso that she hereafter pay the premiums. A day later they asked for the policy's return, delivering in its place a promissory note with a four-month deadline. Having turned over the six hundred dollars, her entire liquid capital, Eliza Enochs insisted that food be sent for — the entire group had been existing on a near starvation diet. When none was forthcoming she grew worried and confided in the landlady.

She had met Mrs. Martin only a short time ago in Nashville, Tennessee, she said. Mrs. Martin, on learning that Eliza wanted to be independent of her wealthy family, straightway proposed that she accompany her to New York. There she could become her assistant in conducting a fashionable female academy about to open.

"There is a train leaving for New York in a half hour,"

Mrs. Martin had said, "and if you care to take the position I offer, you must leave here with me now. I will pay you a hundred dollars a month to start with but under no consideration will I permit you to dally. It is now or never."

So forceful and persuasive was the elderly woman that the young girl, in a plain street dress and raincoat, boarded the train with her and arrived in New York in early February of the current year. During the trip her new-found mentor spoke of the glorious sights she would see in the city while waiting for the academy to open. Once settled in the 23rd Street room, however, she was seldom permitted to leave, and then only when accompanied by one of the women in black. Talk of the female academy gradually faded away.

Hearing this story, the landlady took the initiative. She wired R. W. Enochs at his lumber concern in Mississippi. Somehow the women got wind of the wealthy brother's impending visit. They escorted Eliza Enochs to Hoboken, New Jersey, on the pretext of going to visit Southern friends in that city. When the brother appeared at the 23rd Street boardinghouse, he learned all the circumstances from the landlady, whom he paid in full for the back rental. He then sought out his sister in Hoboken, whisked her unceremoniously out of the hands of her guardians, and returned with her to the South.

Another attempt by the sisters to secure funds involved the Emma Willard Association, composed of former students and supporters of the Willard Seminary in Troy, New York. The association secretary told police Virginia Wardlaw had become a member some years ago. She and her sisters had one great aim in life, she had said at the time — to obtain a large endowment from wealthy Northerners for a school in the South. Once elected to membership, Miss Wardlaw and one of her sisters approached the wealthy

Mrs. Russell Sage, president of the association, and asked her to take a financial interest in their project. Since the soliciting of funds violated the purpose of the association, Virginia Wardlaw was dropped from the membership rolls.

The aged grandmother was the central figure in the account of Mrs. Anna Whitlamb of 977 Flatbush Avenue, Brooklyn. In the spring of the current year, said Mrs. Whitlamb, a veiled woman in black came and asked for accommodations for "an old lady" who was staying at a hotel on the corner. Arrangements were made and the guest was installed.

"The old woman was deathly afraid of the younger one and trembled every time she came to the house," said Mrs. Whitlamb. "The woman in black at first identified herself as Mrs. Martin but I am convinced she was Virginia Wardlaw. At first I didn't know the relationship between her and the aged woman, the younger one claiming to be a trained nurse. One day the aged one accidentally mentioned her daughter and then begged me not to let it be known she had told me. There was no money coming in, so I taxed the alleged nurse and she admitted she was the daughter. She also told me she was nursing a sick girl named Mrs. Snead. I could not find out where she was staying with this girl and when I asked what to do if her mother had trouble she said she was staying in a little house near the sawmill in Flatlands."

The most extraordinary aspects of the visits of the woman in black were their timing — always late at night, with the departure occurring about four in the morning — and the upsetting effect on the aged tenant. "One day I asked the old woman why she feared her daughter," Mrs. Whitlamb continued, "and she replied, 'I would like to tell you. I could tell a lot, but I am afraid of her. She has taken my money and I had a heap of it. I can't take care of myself and she just sticks me around anywhere until she carries out her schemes.'"

That very evening, the troublesome visitor arrived at ten o'clock. Mrs. Whitlamb heard a noise in the room, went into the hallway, and stood outside the door unabashedly eavesdropping. To her ears came the sound of the old woman crying, remonstrances from her visitor, then a full-scale argument.

"It's terrible. It's terrible," Mrs. Whitlamb allegedly heard the old woman say. "What are you planning to do? I know all about you and I don't want a cent of the money if you propose to get it that way. I would rather die now."

The daughter's rough answer came through the door: "Well, you just never mind. If you get any of it at all, you will take it the way I get it and it won't be very long until I get it. She won't live long."

The next day the agitated grandmother wanted to borrow a pen to write a letter, ostensibly to her son in the South who would get her out of "this terrible thing." One of the other boarders gave her a pen and she scrawled a few lines with difficulty. Mrs. Whitlamb said she doubted the letter was ever mailed. When the daughter arrived again a few days later, the landlady demanded the rent, which had never been paid. On previous occasions the woman had whipped out a batch of insurance policies, declaring that there was no cause for worry since someone in the family was about to die and money would be plentiful. Now the insurance policies were again brought forth. Mrs. Whitlamb was adamant about payment of the rent, however, and evicted her tenant.

Along with the stories which accented the need for money came others which suggested studied neglect of the ailing Ocey Snead, and her fear of her guardians. A next-door neighbor of 466 West 22nd Street told of meeting Ocey

Snead and two of the women in black when they came to her house in June, inquiring about rooms in the area. "I saw that the girl was in a delicate condition," this witness related, "and asked them all to stay at my home for dinner. This they did. The initials on a suitcase they carried had been scratched off but there was a tag on it, 'Macon to New York.' The girl seemed in a daze and before asking a question would look at the two women. She was plainly in fear of them, and my heart went out to the poor thing. We began talking about the South, for I knew by their accent where they were from, and the woman I now know was Miss Wardlaw said they had just come from Macon, Georgia, and that they were relatives of the famous Wardlaw family. I knew of the family and told them so, but that was all they would say about themselves."

At 146 Henry Street, landlady Alice J. Wiley recalled that in the past October Ocey Snead and two of her aunts had stayed in her boardinghouse. To her their actions seemed extremely queer, especially the fact that Ocey was often shut up in the bathroom for long periods. On one occasion when she was kept there an entire day, the landlady caught the two women carrying toast and coffee to her. This suspicious behavior caused Mrs. Wiley to order them out of the house.

A new wave of physicians came forth to describe their strange experiences with the family. Dr. Gamble O'Malley of 2809 Clarendon Road, Flatbush, told of being called to attend Martha Eliza Wardlaw in September 1908. Mrs. Wardlaw, partially blind, was treated for a minor ailment. Two weeks later Dr. O'Malley returned to treat Ocey Snead for an attack of tonsillitis. In the Brooklyn house on East 48th Street the family had hardly the actual necessities of existence. When Dr. O'Malley remarked on this, it was explained that they had had much trouble with storage people, that one company had stolen many of their things, including a trunk containing the trousseau of Ocey Snead. The latter related that she and her husband had but recently come from Tennessee, that her husband was currently employed with the Corbin Construction Company, a building contracting firm. Dr. O'Malley, noting that the grandmother had cataracts, ordered the shades pulled down and the blinds drawn.

A more shocking revelation came from Dr. Cornelius Love, of 167 Clinton Street, Brooklyn. In early September of the current year the physician had been called to the Hotel St. George, on Clark Street in Brooklyn. There he had found Ocey Snead in bed. After examining her, he concluded there was nothing organically wrong. She was apparently recovering from childbirth, appeared somewhat anemic, and needed more food. He made his recommendations, including milk and eggs in the diet, and wrote out prescriptions for medicine. He called again a few days later only to find Ocey and her guardian gone. He traced them to 146 Henry Street. There he learned the medicines had not been secured. His patient was in an unexpected condition which puzzled him greatly. Ocey Snead lay in bed almost unconscious, staring at the ceiling in a dazed, fixed manner, as though in a hypnotic trance or under the influence of some opiate. Her eyes were dilated, her heart action irregular. To the elderly women in black attending her, Dr. Love expressed his outrage.

"You have drugged this patient," he admonished. "You must not do it again. You must stop it. Do you want to kill her? If you don't, you must stop giving her this drug."

The two women in attendance denied having done anything to induce Ocey Snead's condition of semitorpor, the one suggesting her condition was such that no doctor could help her. When Dr. Love asked the name and whereabouts of his patient's husband, this woman curtly told him, "We do not like to talk about ourselves." Because he was otherwise engaged, Dr. Love asked another doctor, John Wilkie of 40 Schermerhorn Street, Brooklyn, to check back. Dr. Wilkie also prescribed medicines. When he found that they were never ordered, he decided it was a case to steer clear of and discontinued his calls.

The concern with Ocey Snead's state of health, with her insurance policies, and with her will — or rather wills, for there seemed to be literally dozens in existence — must have been almost a full-time occupation for the three sisters, police surmised. In March of the current year one of the women in black, thought to be either Caroline Martin or Virginia Wardlaw, but more likely the latter, was said to have entered King's clothing store at Sixth Avenue and 23rd Street, Manhattan, accompanied by a young woman. The older woman asked to see the proprietor, but in his absence was forced to settle for clerk Charles Jacobs. Jacobs told police of the encounter.

"This is my niece, who has had trouble with her husband. He has left her," he reported the woman as saying. "She owns considerable property and is in delicate health. She does not want him to get any of the property and is leaving it all to her grandmother."

The young woman appeared to Jacobs to have something the matter with her, to be under a hypnotic spell. Together, the two made a most bizarre impression on him. When they asked him to witness a will, together with two other clerks, he and his companions, who had been observing the scene, all regarded it as a joke. They started to sign, noting that the document already bore the signature "Ocey W. M. Snead." When Jacobs asked the young woman if it was her last will and testament, she said nothing, keeping her eyes fixed on the floor. He repeated the question. This time the elder woman said, "Of course it is," and shook her companion's arm. "Say yes," she demanded and the girl nodded her head. To the further question of why had they not gone to a notary, the older woman replied that they were strangers in the area, and the present signatures were just as valid. With this, she escorted her silent companion out of the store.

Jacobs had come forth when he recognized the women's photos in newspaper accounts. The actual document described turned up in the maze of papers found in Dr. Collins's Third Avenue drugstore several days earlier:

I, Ocey W. M. Snead, of the borough of Brooklyn, city of New York, make public and declare this my last will and testament, revoking all my real estate, amounting to four acres, comprising sixteen (16) lots in block twenty nine (29), Wilder Park, Jefferson County, Louisville, Kentucky, that were sold by Ruth S. Collins, commonly known as the Martin Block, together with all improvements thereon. Said four acres being particularly described in the recording deed from Ruth S. Collins to the said Caroline B. Martin. Said four acres composing the entire block 29, bounded on the south by Highland Boulevard, on the north by Young Street, on the west by Wilder Avenue, and on the east by a street parallel to Third Street, said block 29 containing the whole of the original 16 lots or four acres sold by Ruth S. Collins to Caroline B. Martin. I appoint the said Martha Eliza Wardlaw sole executrix and direct that no bond or security be recognized in testament thereof. I hereby subscribe this instrument on the eleventh day of March, A.D. nineteen hundred and nine.

OCEY W. M. SNEAD

Police authorities, fortified by the material snowballing into their hands, felt their case tightening. In fact, they let it be known that in their view, not only was Virginia Wardlaw guilty of murder but her sisters, Mary Snead and the missing Caroline Martin, were probably accomplices, partners in a hideous conspiracy.

Lawyer Franklin Fort scoffed at these charges. The countless wills proved nothing, he said. Once he had had a client who made out nine wills in as many days. The concern for Ocey Snead's welfare was clearly demonstrated, not negated, by the continuing calls for medical assistance. If the family relied on an old-fashioned approach to health, refusing to yield to the instructions of physicians, that was a peculiarity perhaps, but not a criminal failing. All the Wardlaw women were innocent, he insisted, their insurance maneuverings a desperate effort to escape total financial eclipse. Typical of the faulty information reaching the press and police, he asserted, was the attempt to show ill feeling between his client, Virginia Wardlaw, and her mother. To refute this implication, he released a fragment of a poem in his possession. Composed by Martha Eliza Wardlaw, it was entitled "Resurrection of a Sacred Nursery on Lord's Day in December 1908 — Christmastide." The verses conveyed a tender memory picture of her children, especially a trio which included Virginia, described as having only "one aim in life — unselfish love." The lines also spoke of "Johnnie boy," the Princetonian Wardlaw who died young; and of "my youngest boy," who "father-like did pulpit choose" — this being Albert, said to be in the South. In later years, said the verse, another daughter, Bessie, brought joy, which was dimmed, however, by the sorrows of the Civil War. The poem was signed "Mother (M.E.W.)."

. . . .
The trundle bed was soon in place
with cherubs three of radiant face.
My Johnnie boy did win high fame

and honored well his father's name.
My youngest boy stepped in his shoes,
and father-like did pulpit choose.
The little sister, as she grew,
one aim in life she only knew —
Unselfish love she proved so true
in all she ever sought to do.
The phonograph echoes its sway
as Truth these three sent on its way,
To form from each a lasting ray,
to shine for e'er in endless day.
Our Bessie came in later years,
her brightness mingled joy with tears.
The Civil War brought want and woe.
The tale is told just o'er and o'er.
Oh, may her life of coming years
ne'er know her mother's flowing tears!
Though eighty years do claim me now,
these pictures move so bright, somehow.

Mary Snead, too, attempted to refute what she called the false reports circulated. "In the first place, there is the report that Mrs. Wardlaw was afraid of her daughter. This is absolutely false," she said firmly. "The mother and daughter were a loving pair, and Miss Wardlaw continually did everything in her power to make her mother happy and comfortable. I would like to say why the house in Flatlands came to be surrounded by so much mystery. For two months before we went to East Orange we were living at different places and the Flatlands house was closed. We went there from time to time to get mail, and that is what gave it such a mysterious aspect. It was closed up. When Ocey's baby was ill I called on Mrs. Wardlaw and told her of it. Some person must have overheard enough to know that someone would die and then made the rest of the story up out of whole cloth."

To counter the impression that Ocey Snead feared her aunts, Fort produced a letter she had written from New York to *My Darling Tante,* signifying her Aunt Virginia, in 1901. Mary Snead, also spoken of in the letter, was referred to as "Aunt Mamie."

My darling Tante,

Mother arrived this afternoon and delighted my heart with your kind message about the ring that you are going to give me and the kindly mention that you and dear Aunt Mamie and the teachers and pupils of Soule College have made of me during the visit to that dear home that I love so dearly. I am sorry she did not see grandma and still more sorry that I cannot see her with my own eyes, for I love her more than almost anybody in the world. Upon her arrival mother received the letter from you, which came after she started. Mother begs that you go to the guest chamber and sleep alone to prevent draining your nerve vitality during the night for at least a few nights until you get your brain thoroughly rested and take a little extra brain nourishment, such as cocoa and Sarsaparilla, to benefit your blood, and move your desk into a light corner on account of your eyes and let someone else decide the yes and no of many minor matters which have piled up on top of the great matters that have fatigued your dear, precious brain to the point of extreme danger of permanent nervous prostration, which gives me unutterable solicitude. Don't be offended at my suggestion about your health, which is priceless to you and to all who love you. You should take this rest now before you begin the nervous strain of commencement, and so that you will not be visibly gone to pieces before your audiences. Your

brother John overworked himself and ruined a brilliant
mind, and you will do the same unless you pause and rest.
With all the devotion of which the human heart is capable, I
am your devoted niece,

OCEY WARDLAW MARTIN

The matter of inquiries about the size of bathtubs was
another area of misconceptions, said Fort. Caroline Martin
often stayed with her sisters and she was a stout woman.
Naturally, a large bathtub was needed, though in fact the
one in East Orange was only four feet in length. As for the
tale of a Negro coming to the East Orange house, it was
simply groundless.

Prosecutor Wilbur Mott said he also discounted the incidents involving a Negro man. His office issued a statement
which made another minor concession: "We are convinced
from letters and papers we have seen that Mrs. Martha Eliza
Wardlaw, the grandmother of Ocey Snead and beneficiary
under her life insurance policies, was not a party to a plot to
bring about the young woman's death."

10

THE OBJECT OF SO MUCH DIZZYING ACTIVITY LAY STILL, meanwhile, in the East Orange undertaking establishment of Gustave Kunz. A second autopsy was performed by County
Physician McKenzie and his assistant Dr. Simmons. All vital
organs were removed for examination by Dr. William H.
Hicks, an expert chemist and pathologist. After studying the
brain, Hicks said the victim could not have died of cerebral
hemorrhage.

"The young woman suffered from no organic trouble," summed up McKenzie. "If she had received the proper amount of food she doubtless would have been alive today. The condition of the intestines proves conclusively that she suffered from starvation. At the time of death she weighed less than eighty pounds. It's a plain case of murder — nothing else. We are almost certain that either a poison or an opiate was given to the young woman just before she was placed in the bathtub. When I say the young woman was placed in the bathtub, I mean that Ocey Snead in her weakened condition was not able to walk from the bed to the tub or even attempt to take a bath. She was carried there and placed in the water to drown."

It was also possible, suggested Simmons, that a little whiskey might have been used to prevent resistance. Both New Jersey and New York authorities checked their files. There was no recorded instance of a suicide by drowning.

As preparations were made for the body's burial the case took a surprising detour. The insurance companies, asked by Franklin Fort to advance money to pay for funeral expenses, flatly refused to do so. They were not convinced, they said, that the body in the morgue was that of Ocey Snead. To support their contention they produced Neil Campbell, who happened to be an insurance man himself, though not with either Equitable or New York Life, the two firms contacted.

Campbell's home in Brooklyn was only four doors away from the House of Mystery. He reported that several times in August he had seen a young woman, beautifully dressed and corresponding in height and appearance to photos of Ocey Snead, entering number 1693, always in the dead of night and accompanied by a man he believed to be Fletcher Snead. Arriving in a red touring car, the couple apparently stayed inside for several hours but departed before daylight. Once, Campbell stated, the girl rang the doorbell and there was no response. After beating frantically at the front window she went away.

Another neighbor, Mrs. Joseph Johnson, who had been called upon to photograph Ocey Snead, also reported seeing a double of the sick girl.

Faced with the insurance companies' position, Prosecutor Mott ordered the body embalmed and held. Meanwhile he sent for Dr. William Pettit to identify the patient he had once treated. "My heavens, this girl must have been subjected to inhuman treatment," the Brooklyn physician exclaimed after his examination. "The stitches taken in the wound months ago have not been removed. I called at the house in Brooklyn several times for the express purpose of removing these stitches, but each time was denied admission."

Dr. Pettit was next taken to the Essex County Jail to make sure the woman there was Virginia Wardlaw. "She was as unconcerned as a schoolgirl," he reported after the brief visit. "But she was the nurse who declined or neglected to obey my instructions when attending her niece." It was his view, he declared, that a murder had been committed and a drug used in the process. This explanation was made more likely by the autopsy result which showed that there was little water in the stomach; a normal person would tend to swallow a good deal in drowning. Dr. Pettit recalled that he had once seen a bottle of chloroform on the mantel in the Brooklyn house. When he asked about it, Virginia Wardlaw, with what he described as a "ghastly smile," said simply, "Oh, maybe we wanted it for you, doctor."

A second identification was made by the Reverend John A. McCague, of the Old First Presbyterian Church at Fifth Avenue and Eleventh Street, Manhattan. The pastor recalled Ocey Snead from the time of her first child's birth, in early February 1908. He had baptized little Mary Alberta.

Several days later, on February 13, it had been his sad duty to officiate at the baby's funeral. The services took place in a Broadway hotel of good standing. Prior to moving there, Ocey and Fletcher Snead had received him at their fashionable East Eleventh Street apartment. At first they seemed to have a good deal of money. Their social standing was such that they were readily recognized by the members of his church, in which Ocey had been active, assisting in the Sunday school and acting as a substitute teacher of a kindergarten class. Later, McCague said, they had apparently fallen on bad times. One of Ocey's aunts, a Mrs. Martin, had come to him with a plan to organize a fresh-air home on a plantation she said she owned in Virginia. She wanted McCague to allow her to solicit funds, up to ten thousand dollars, from the congregation. The pastor had refused her request on the grounds that it was against church rules to canvass for funds.

When, despite these identifications, the insurance companies still refused to advance payment pending complete disposition of the case, Franklin Fort proposed to handle expenses out of his own pocket. At this point, Wilbur Mott said a contingency fund from his office would be made available for the purpose. Among his team, the prosecutor said, there was great sympathy for Ocey Snead. It was his hope, he added, that the funeral would at last flush out of hiding the dead girl's mother, the missing Caroline Martin.

From 11 to 12 A.M. on Tuesday, December 7, the body of Ocey Snead was on public view, gazed at by strands of curiosity seekers who filed through the East Orange morgue. The dead girl's face appeared thin and drawn, but with distinct vestiges of beauty in the fine features and in the long luxuriant hair woven into a graceful pattern around her brow. Draped over the lower half of the simple gray coffin was a cloth of silver gray. The coffin itself was trimmed with handles of silver and a silver plate inscribed *Ocey W. M. Snead*. The only floral remembrance was a small bouquet of forget-me-nots and lilies. It had been given the previous day by total strangers, a former East Orange alderman and his wife who had ordered it on learning no relatives or friends had sent anything.

At noon, the Reverend John F. Kern, pastor of the German Presbyterian Church, hurried through a verse of scripture and recited the Lord's Prayer. A scant score of people were in attendance. Four professional mourners carried the casket to a waiting wagon, which took it to the Lackawanna Railroad station. From there it was to go to Hoboken, New Jersey, then across the North River to 23rd Street in Manhattan, passing within a block of the lodgings of Mary Snead before boarding a Putnam Railroad car headed for Eighth Avenue and West 155th Street.

Hardly had the casket left the East Orange morgue when Franklin Fort arrived. He demanded to know why the service had been held ahead of the schedule announced to him. The funeral was a county affair, he was told, and as such held whenever the people on the scene felt it fit to do so. The lawyer's anger increased when he learned that Virginia Wardlaw had pleaded for one last look at her "little girl" and had been refused.

Fort protested the "cruelty" of that denial before taking a cab to 466 West 22nd Street. With Mary Snead at his side, he continued to West 155th Street, stopping to buy a bouquet of flowers and arriving in time to meet the train bearing the casket. From the station it was only a quarter mile to Mount Hope Cemetery. The body was carried in an ancient hearse drawn by a single black horse. The aunt and Fort followed in a small four-wheeled chaise, behind them a straggling group of newsmen and photographers.

At the graveside, Mary Snead leaned heavily on the arm

of Franklin Fort. All in black, she was voluminously veiled. As the undertaker in a singsong voice repeated, "In the name of the Father and of the Son and of the Holy Ghost. Amen," her shoulders shook visibly. With a handkerchief she dabbed at the moistened veils, unable to restrain her sobs. The undertaker's sonorous voice repeated the Lord's Prayer. The brief service was over. At a signal four laborers gripped the casket and Ocey Snead's wasted body was lowered into the grave. Here it rested next to those of her first-born, Mary Alberta, and her father, Colonel Robert Martin. Mary Snead waited until the ground had been filled in, gently placed a small bunch of calla lilies on the fresh earth, and walked slowly away.

She was the only relative to brave the windswept slopes of Mount Hope. Why had maternal love not driven Ocey's mother to the graveside, reporters asked. In New York she would presumably have been immune from arrest. Franklin Fort gave a partial answer when he said he had asked authorities to permit a private service in a chapel, with guaranteed immunity from arrest, but had been refused. Did he know the mother's whereabouts? He would not say that he did, replied Fort, nor that he did not. Why did she consider it necessary to conceal herself in this way? "That is a hard question to answer," said the lawyer. "Perhaps she could accomplish more in some other direction."

Like Fort, Mary Snead felt that there were undoubtedly good reasons why Mrs. Martin had not come to the funeral. It was her sister Virginia, however, who caused her the greatest concern. "It is awful that an innocent woman should be crushed beneath the heels of a false public opinion — to be sent to her death," she said. "We had many friends in the South, and many enemies in Murfreesboro who are inspiring the false statements coming from there. Many years ago, Miss Wardlaw was done an unspeakable wrong — I won't tell you what it was — by these same enemies who are now sending out the terrible lies about us all. It's shameful! Shameful!"

11

OVER THE WEEKEND dispatches had been filtering north from Virginia and Tennessee, accounts of the three sisters' lives in the South which could only be described as hair-raising. In the small town mentioned by Mary Snead, Murfreesboro, Tennessee, all the residents recalled the black-garbed clan, regarded by them as weird, eccentric, and sinister. Little Ocey seemed to be a virtual prisoner, called "Ocey" although she was said to hate that name, forced by the sisters to marry her own cousin against her will, subjected to strange influences. "From the moment we learned that they had placed a policy for upwards of fifteen thousand dollars on the young life of Ocey Martin we knew she was doomed," said Mayor J. H. Chrichlow, summing up the town's attitude.

The background of the stories had their origin, as with so many tales of the South, in the Civil War. The eldest of the three sisters, Caroline, was born in 1845; Mary three years later, and Virginia in 1852. All three were thus young adolescents during the bloody years of that struggle which ravaged the countryside, reducing once proud and wealthy families to humiliating indigence. Despite severe losses, the Wardlaw family slowly regained its footing. Each cent the father was able to put aside went for the education of his children. All three sisters attended good schools in the South, Virginia later going north to become a charter stu-

dent at the newly founded Wellesley College. All three subsequently became highly respected teachers. Caroline taught
first near her home and later in private and public schools in
New York. Similarly, Mary taught in the South and also at
Dr. Norman's private school on West 62nd Street in New
York City. Virginia taught at the Price School in Nashville
and established a glowing reputation for her progressive
methods of instruction.

It was in 1892 that a prominent Nashville banker, Samuel
J. Keith, asked her to accept the presidency of Murfreesboro's Soule Female College, on whose board he served. The
offer was a signal honor. Soule, founded in 1851 and named
for Methodist Bishop Joseph Soule, was the earliest college
to be established in Rutherford County and one of the finest
educational institutions in the South. Its prospectus
promised knowledge "through education of the heart and
mind, without that superficial gaudy show, to the neglect of
the impartation of sound and useful knowledge and the
training, too, of the mind to a proper degree of thinking
and reasoning, which is but too characteristic of female
schools. . . . Those who wish their children to obtain simply the art of talking nonsense and showing off in superficial
tinsel had better not send them to Murfreesboro, for here
they will be compelled to study, or be exposed at the crucial
moment."

A typical advertisement offered: *Higher Education for
Women. Full College Course. Frequent Stereopticon illustrations on subjects studied. French, German, and Italian
spoken and taught. Education, Art, Dress-Making, Book-
keeping, Typewriting, Commercial Law. Lectures by Vanderbilt Professors.*

Murfreesboro, a highly cultured little town with an in-
tensely Southern atmosphere, would certainly have held
considerable appeal for the new college president. Its liter-

ary heritage included the works of local colorists, Mary
Noailles Murfree, a member of the town's founding family
who wrote under the name of Charles Egbert Craddock,
and another woman writer, Will Allen Dromgoole. From
1819 to 1825, Murfreesboro was the capital of Tennessee.
Thereafter it remained the permanent county seat of Rutherford County. During the Civil War a bloody battle involving ninety thousand blue- and gray-clad soldiers took place
along Stones River just outside the town. For three days the
fighting raged, spilling out into the countryside. By the time
the guns quieted, a wide radius around the town had been
turned into a wild and dreary waste, the college buildings at
Soule into a hospital where wounded and dying soldiers lay
in converted classrooms, their tattered uniforms drenched in
blood.

Recovery came, made possible by the fertile farmland of
the area. Fields of cotton and corn grew once more, joined
later by golden pumpkins which dotted the ground. Rich in
wildflowers, the countryside was alive with violets, anem-
ones, shooting stars, and pinkroot. Red dogwood added
its bright luster in season, as did redbuds or Judas trees
with their rose and white blossoms and the wild plum;
in the fall resplendent maples were afire with color. Man-
sions with names like Bloomfield, Bellwood, Oak Manor,
Riverside, and Marymount were restored, their life less gay
than in antebellum days but nonetheless gentle and gra-
cious. Distinguished visitors, including the former president
of the Confederacy, Jefferson Davis, came to stay with
friends or relatives in the area. Murfreesboro, by now a
relaxed town of about four thousand residents, was the center of the region's activities, proud of its fine stores, its
churches, its well-cared-for square, and its thriving college,
Soule, home of fourteen instructors and over two hundred
students.

Soon after being installed as president, Virginia Wardlaw sent for her mother and father, who had retired after many years of service with the Georgia Methodist Conference. They stayed with her for a time, then moved to a cottage in town where the respected old preacher died in 1896. Within the year, Mary Snead, recently become a widow, came to town with her three sons Fletcher, John, and Albert. Mary taught at the college, where she was well liked. Virginia, too, taught classes. Her pleasant cultivated manner and inventive management kept the Soule dormitories filled to capacity. Townspeople who met her were impressed by her brilliant conversation. The sisters' black dress was remarked upon. Certainly they were considered somewhat eccentric, but they were also august and inscrutable. In the South, where strange legends abound and original behavior amuses and fascinates, the wearing of black added to the occultness of the pair, inspiring respect and awe rather than ridicule.

Everyone agreed that matters were going along very smoothly, for nine highly profitable years, until the arrival in Murfreesboro of the eldest sister in 1901. At first, Caroline Martin seemed an attractive addition to the family, a witty, forceful figure clad always in the family black, veiled, wearing the black fingerless gloves popular a generation past. With her came her daughter, sixteen-year-old Ocey Wardlaw Martin, a lovely girl who quickly became everyone's favorite. Ocey registered at the school and became an excellent student.

Slowly, almost imperceptibly, however, conditions at the flourishing college began to change. Mrs. Martin became the dominant spirit of the institution. Although extremely entertaining and persuasive at times, other occasions found her ruling with a rod of iron, harsh and abrupt. She seldom spoke of her husband, Colonel Martin, who had died recently in New York, but she never hesitated to refer glibly to prominent connections in that city, people with names like Vanderbilt, Astor, and Mrs. Russell Sage, philanthropist wife of the railroad tycoon. All business transactions at the school were gradually taken over by the eldest sister. Money flowed freely through her hands. The impression she gave was of having an unlimited supply.

When bills incurred by the college fell months behind in payment, townspeople became suspicious. They wondered why even Virginia Wardlaw, the president, dared not contradict her sister, why she submitted blindly to her every demand. What was her hold? Was there some dark secret which only she knew? The remarkable similarity in appearance of little Ocey and her aunt Virginia was now remarked upon. In whispers, the people of Murfreesboro asked themselves if Ocey was not actually Virginia's daughter, raised by Caroline Martin to protect her maiden sister's name.

Suddenly little Ocey stopped attending classes. The girl had the measles, her mother said, but when the illness extended beyond a month, stretched from spring through summer, the whispers grew. Why was the young student, previously so gay and sweet-natured, confined to her room for such long periods? Apprehension grew when it was learned that an insurance policy of seven thousand dollars was being taken out for Ocey.

Townspeople now feared for her life and suspected she was being slowly poisoned. They insisted that she receive medical attention and a physician was sent for. He was not permitted inside the sickroom. Ocey, pale and wan, was brought out to the hallway on a cot. Here the doctor made his diagnosis, which revealed no serious illness, and wrote out prescriptions. Ocey reappeared from time to time, but soon another period of illness would cause her renewed withdrawal.

At the school a precipitous decline was underway, its origin a breakdown of morale. Girls were being changed from room to room without reason. Living on the premises, the three sisters were constantly seen roaming about the buildings, wandering mysteriously through classrooms and down hallways past the dormitory rooms. Often students at play in the courtyard would be startled by the apparition of Mrs. Martin glaring down at them from a high window.

One night a student awoke with a fright to see all three gathered around the stove in her room, mumbling and chanting. The next morning it was explained that they had smelled something burning and had come to investigate. On another occasion this same student, after a late tutorial meeting, was invited by Virginia Wardlaw to rest in her room rather than return to her own. All night, the student recalled, the school president would sigh in her sleep and say, "My God! My God! My sister!"

From other sources came similar accounts of unorthodox behavior. Hack drivers reported that the sisters would send for a carriage, always at night, and drive to the local cemetery. There they would hover around a gravestone and talk in low tones for hours. Negro drivers would refuse to answer their nocturnal calls and eventually, it was said, the calls were abandoned.

One Murfreesboro resident, on business in nearby Nashville, told of seeing a woman on the street, dowdy, shabbily dressed, who yet reminded him of someone he knew. Taking a second look, he was amazed to recognize Virginia Wardlaw. He watched as she met a young man carrying a suitcase, entered a hack with him, took out of the case a black hat of good quality, and exchanged it for the ancient bonnet she had worn earlier. A fresh cape replaced the old garment worn on the street. Once again she was the dignified president of Soule College.

Small-town imaginations no doubt embroidered on some

of these tales, but their essence, the eccentricity of the three women in black, clearly bore substance. Soon perplexed students were deserting Soule College in large numbers; discipline among those who remained was collapsing completely; money matters were in a state of chaos. Finally a committee of trustees took charge, ousting the three sisters. But the damage done proved irreparable. After trying for several years to restore Soule to its former eminence, a new administration gave up. The main building was sold to the town, which tore it down and erected a public school on the site.

The sisters did not immediately leave Murfreesboro. They moved into an old house on North Maple Street, the residence of a Confederate veteran, Colonel A. Searcy. Here their behavior became an unending source of town gossip. In two large rooms on the second floor, all three set up housekeeping, along with the ailing Ocey. No one was admitted to the rooms; no one knew how they were furnished. The blinds were always down. Only at night did the three sisters venture forth, trailing their long black capes, seemingly in perpetual mourning, whether for those already dead or those about to die no one ever knew.

The sisters' mania for leaving packages and storing things was much remarked upon. On one occasion Caroline Martin asked to store a number of household items in a room of a private residence. Soon she reappeared, asking to do some writing on a desk among these possessions. To the amazement of the owner of the house, she proceeded to settle herself among the clutter, apparently working through files of papers, even receiving visits from her sisters before moving out again days later.

While the sons of Mary Snead maintained a separate residence, Fletcher Snead paid one long visit to the Searcy house, much commented on in the town. "When we first saw

Fletcher Snead enter the house he was smooth-shaven," Colonel Searcy recalled. "Three months later, when he left the place for the first time, he wore a full beard. We could hear the click of his typewriter all the time, but he never showed his face outside of his room, and we were never able to get a peep inside."

Another time, a former business associate and army comrade of Colonel Martin called at the North Maple Street house. Captain Headly, passing through the region with his wife, had decided to break up the trip by calling on their old friends. Mrs. Headly was particularly eager to see Ocey, whom she had known as a young child. Caroline Martin came downstairs to greet them, chatted amiably on the porch, but to their surprise did not invite them in. When the Headlys asked about Ocey, they were told she was too ill to receive visitors. The news, together with the puzzling porch reception, made the visitors suspicious. They insisted on seeing the girl, even if only for a moment. Sensing their determination, Mrs. Martin retreated upstairs, returning a moment later reinforced by Virginia Wardlaw. The latter also tried to deter the Headlys. Finally she led the determined couple upstairs. In a poorly furnished bedroom they saw a languid Ocey, who acknowledged them with scant enthusiasm. To their inquiries, she replied that she was not ill, felt no pain, was "just drowsy." The Headlys both sensed a sinister influence at work, a force which they could not define. Not knowing what to do, however, they left, uneasy and unhappy with their visit.

Mayor Chrichlow, settling a business matter relating to Soule College, paid one call at the mysterious dwelling on North Maple Street. "The house was in utter darkness when I got there," he recalled. "Finally they led me to a curtained-off space, behind which Miss Wardlaw was sitting on a couch, her face covered with a veil." The mayor obtained the signature he needed to accomplish his errand, and sped from the premises.

Colonel Searcy recalled only one other visitor, a well-dressed stranger who came to the house asking for the sisters. On this occasion they would not take him to their quarters, but paid the colonel a dollar to temporarily use his parlor.

While the rent on the rooms was sometimes paid, it was usually in arrears. Early in 1905 the ménage suddenly disappeared in the middle of the night, still owing seventy-five dollars. The furniture had been sent to a railroad freight house, shipped and reshipped so that the final destination was hard to ascertain. The sisters themselves had appeared at the local railroad depot and taken a southbound train. As was their wont, they purchased no tickets in the depot, waiting to buy them on the train. Their destination was therefore also unknown.

12

EVENTUALLY IT WAS LEARNED that the raven-clad sisters had dispersed. Mary Snead soon reappeared in Oglethorpe, Georgia, where the family mansion she had once shared with her husband still stood. Townspeople there recalled the Snead family as somewhat original in its unheralded arrivals and departures, the marriage as not very satisfactory. Caroline Martin, accompanied by her daughter, had traveled to New York. And Virginia Wardlaw turned up in Christiansburg, Virginia, where the family had close relatives.

Mrs. Oceana Seaborn Pollock, ninety-three years old, was

the sister of Martha Eliza Wardlaw. In the family tradition, the three sisters' great aunt had for years been a reputable educator, owner and director of the well-regarded Montgomery College. The burden of years was now upon her. With a sense of relief she put her newly arrived niece in charge of that local institution.

For Virginia Wardlaw, her nerves frayed by set-tos with angry creditors and hostile residents of Murfreesboro, the move was equally appealing. Once again she could practice the profession she loved, and in a school with rich traditions, one founded as early as 1850 exclusively for women, and later expanded to include a male academy as well. Instruction for the complete college course was advertised as "exact and thorough." Students boarded and studied in a large rambling old building which had once boasted a spire, the structure's original owner having been the local Presbyterian Church. The grounds were on a hill at the east end of town and were handsomely landscaped to form a congenial setting.

At the foot of the hill, the local cemetery was a reminder of Christiansburg's colorful past. The town was established in 1792 and named for Colonel William Christian, a brother-in-law of Patrick Henry and a member of the Virginia House of Burgesses. Although the population had never gone far beyond a thousand residents, Christiansburg became the seat of Montgomery County. The town with its wide, tree-lined streets, situated in the midst of a prosperous rolling countryside, attracted pioneer families who paused a year or two before going farther west. Daniel Boone, Evan Shelby, Stephen Austin, Davy Crockett, and other kindred spirits were such temporary residents. Another, Major William Clark, was the man who later teamed with Meriwether Lewis on a memorable exploring expedition across the Northwest. A mecca for travelers, the small town boasted fine hotel facilities in its early history. Its courthouse gathered together one of the strongest bars in the state of Virginia. Many present-day inhabitants recalled the Civil War battles that raged in the area, and were fond of telling tales of duels and other customs representative of the past.

In addition to her aged aunt, the new head of Montgomery College had another close relative at hand. Virginia Wardlaw's younger sister Bessie lived in a spacious house two miles outside of town. Her husband Richard Spindle was a prominent businessman of the region. Together, these relatives could provide company and comfort, as well as entree to the society of Christiansburg and that of Roanoke, only thirty miles to the east.

All the omens seemed auspicious, and indeed the reign of the new school head got off to a fine start. The curriculum was updated, the dormitories refurbished. So that full use could be made of the facilities, the school building remained open in the summer, operating as a combination boardinghouse and health resort.

Unfortunately, the good times were destined to be short. Now, as they had in Murfreesboro, the rest of the clan began to gather. Mary Snead arrived first, a quiet passive woman who blended into the new life. One of her sons, Albert, had gone to Colorado and become a rancher. The other two, Fletcher and John, soon followed their mother. They, too, created no problem. With the appearance of Caroline Martin, however, the fabric of the school swiftly disintegrated. The forceful older sister came to town accompanied by her daughter and immediately, as if by royal decree, took over direction of the school.

The subsequent havoc was speedier in Christiansburg than it had been in Murfreesboro. For no apparent reason, Mrs. Martin would change the pattern of courses. Again, students would be shifted from room to room. Padlocks

were put on certain doors, double padlocks and triple padlocks, adding a note of secrecy. As at Soule College, the
three sisters would roam the corridors, startling the residents
with their unexpected sallies.

More disturbing still was the family attitude toward the
two remaining Snead boys, Fletcher and John. Both were
considered mild-mannered, somewhat indecisive, and under
the thumb of their aunts Virginia and Caroline. There was
surprise in Christiansburg, therefore, when they left for
Lynnville, Tennessee, where they opened a sawmill and operated it successfully. At the same time they began courting
the two daughters of J. R. McLaurin, a prominent lawyer. A
double wedding ensued, a child was born to the Fletcher
Sneads, and both couples seemed happy.

Too happy, apparently. In Lynnville, Mrs. Martin suddenly appeared, insisting that John Snead accompany her
back to Christiansburg to take a teaching position at the
school. Young Snead's wife pleaded with him to stay. On
this occasion he held out against the willful aunt, even going
so far as to have police eject her from the house. He reportedly told neighbors he would not allow her to wreck his
home. In a few weeks, the resolute Mrs. Martin reappeared.
On this second visit, John Snead's resolve weakened. He returned to teach at Montgomery, leaving his wife behind.
She wrote him tearful letters but once back in the family
nest, John Snead no longer made the decisions. His wife's
health declined and soon she was placed in a sanitarium.

The young man's spirits also declined rapidly. A strange
series of accidents overtook him. Traveling with Mrs. Martin
near Roanoke, he fell off a train as it was starting to pick up
speed. While he and his aunt claimed that it was an
accident, the brakeman felt he had witnessed a suicide attempt. Several weeks later, M. G. Corello, who lived near
the school, heard an insistent alarm raised by Virginia Ward-

law. Rushing to the scene, he saw John Snead in an open
cistern, from which he pulled him just in time to save his
life. It seemed clear to Corello that the young man was trying to commit suicide. The family explained, however, that
he had fallen into the cistern while taking measurements
with a view to providing a water supply for the school.

A week later it was again Virginia Wardlaw whose cries
brought people running. This time it was eight o'clock in the
morning, the scene John Snead's room in the school building. Two teachers were the first to respond. They saw young
Snead lying on the floor, thrashing about, his night garments
on fire. His aunt was trying to put out the flames. The teachers went to her aid, then called for medical assistance. Three
hours later the twenty-eight-year-old John Snead was dead
of first-degree burns.

One version of his death said his clothing ignited while he
was trying to kindle a fire with kerosene oil. Another version
said a lamp exploded, igniting the bedclothes. Those summoned for assistance, however, insisted they had seen no evidence of an attempt to build a fire, nor had the lamp shown
results of an explosion. All agreed the bedclothes had been
saturated with the kerosene oil. Either, it was whispered,
there had been foul play, or Snead himself had applied a
match for the purpose of self-destruction.

Town gossip inclined toward the former view when it was
heard that the dead man had been heavily insured by his
aunts, that he had recently reassigned one policy from his
absent wife to Virginia Wardlaw as beneficiary. In present-
ing their claims, the women in black maintained that death
was accidental. To support this contention, Virginia can-
vassed the town to obtain supporting affidavits. She met
with no great success, the majority of statements hedging
the crucial point.

The first to render medical assistance, Dr. W. W. Rangeley, said simply, "This is to certify that I attended John B. Wardlaw Snead during his illness which resulted in death. His death was due to a burn." The victim's uncle, Richard Spindle, was similarly noncommittal: "This is to certify that when I was hurriedly called to help Mr. John B. Wardlaw Snead I found the doctors doing everything possible to help him and save his life. Those who reached Mr. Snead before I did have made affidavits that Mr. Snead's death was due to an accident with a kerosene lamp. Of my own personal knowledge I saw nothing contrary to their statement that Mr. John B. Wardlaw Snead's death was accidental."

To establish his brother's soundness of mind, Fletcher Snead was induced to write a letter to the insurance company which concluded as follows: "He was a man of high principle and great fidelity to duty. He was remarkably diligent and economical, although he had handled very great sums of money. Gross injustice has been done to him and to his family in Christiansburg by the allies of your local agent and also in Christiansburg by the allies of his wife's brother, the first actuated by revenge and the second by avarice. I trust that your great company will not lend itself to the calumnies with which these cruel allied persecutors have followed him into Christiansburg and into your very office."

By dint of perseverance the sisters eventually received a favorable insurance settlement.

While his brother was going through his last traumatic months of life, Fletcher Snead was also having difficulties. Again, a visit from Mrs. Martin signaled their start. She came to Lynnville, charging Fletcher to go to Louisville to look after some family property. The next his wife heard from him was a telephone call from Chattanooga, saying he was very sick. Traveling to that city, she was met by Mrs. Martin, who said her nephew was too ill to see anyone. She insisted that Fletcher's wife return to Lynnville and promised that Fletcher would be there shortly. A week later, Fletcher had still not returned home. His wife now made a second trip to Chattanooga, where she found her husband had been moved from one boardinghouse to another by a woman answering to the description of Mrs. Martin. In despair the deserted wife returned home, and eventually obtained a divorce.

To the astonishment of Christiansburg's residents, who had noted no great warmth between them, Fletcher Snead proceeded to marry his first cousin Ocey. And then to confound matters further, he went through a second wedding ceremony. Fletcher, too, was heavily insured, ran the rumor, and there were those who feared he might meet a fate similar to his brother's. And did not Albert Snead, at a distance in Colorado, also carry a heavy insurance load on his head?

Financial difficulties seemed to be at the bottom of the three sisters' far-flung manipulations in the South. Again and again they sought funds by many means, mortgaging real estate, seeking loans on insurance policies or the school property, trying to interest wealthy men in joining them as partners. The encounters with prominent businessmen were innumerable and not easily forgotten by them.

John L. Vaughan, a bank president in Redford, Virginia, remembered a telephone call in which he was told that persons from New York were anxious to discuss with him a large real estate transaction. He agreed to meet with the party. A carriage drove up bearing three women in black. Although it was a warm summer day, the curtains were drawn and the storm robe was up in front. The eldest of the three, a Mrs. Martin, handed Vaughan a bundle wrapped in a newspaper. They wanted the contents to go to him, she said. When he opened it, Vaughan found twelve hundred dollars in paper money. They wished to offer him this sum for his influence and name in connection with Montgomery College,

Mrs. Martin explained. The puzzled banker refused to take the money.

At the women's insistence, Vaughan entered the carriage to go to Christiansburg and look over the property. On arriving, he was taken by Virginia Wardlaw into a room with a red carpet. This was the "Red Room," she said proudly, and he might make it his home in the future, should he consent to serve as dean of the school. After inspecting the rest of the property, Vaughan was asked his opinion as to the cost of putting the college back into shape. He gave an estimate. If he lent them this amount, he was told, they would happily pay twenty per cent interest. They actually had plenty of money themselves, said Mrs. Martin, and proceeded to prove it. From a trash barrel she pulled out a roll of bills covered with ashes. There was more than seven thousand dollars about the house, she declared, adding that she kept the money there because she did not trust banks.

Intrigued by his companions, Vaughan agreed to take dinner and spend the night. In the morning he left, unwilling to put up the requested loan because he felt the sisters did not have the proper collateral. Thereafter, he and his bank were besieged by demands for money under an endless variety of conditions.

C. T. Jennings, owner of a piano salesroom on Campbell Avenue in Roanoke, told of a telephone call which summoned him to the Hotel Roanoke, ostensibly to meet someone who desired to purchase pianos. No name was given. Jennings thought it was a queer procedure but decided to try it out. Following instructions, he presented himself at the hotel, walking into the palm court lobby. Without a word, a tall, elderly woman dressed in black got up from a chair at the window. She escorted Jennings out of the hotel and around the corner to a private home.

"There I was asked to wait until my strange companion

had ascertained that all was in readiness for my reception," the businessman recalled. "Not a word of explanation had been given me, but after waiting several minutes I was admitted into the presence of a woman whom I afterward learned to be Mrs. Martin. The other woman was Miss Wardlaw. According to the scheme they outlined to me, plans had been made for the consolidation of Montgomery College at Christiansburg and Roanoke College at Salem, one of the oldest institutions in the South. The new pianos were to be delivered upon reorganization. It appeared, however, that they first wanted to dispose of the old instruments at Christiansburg. There were four uprights, three squares, and one organ, and they wanted four hundred dollars for them. I agreed to give them two hundred dollars on the pianos and advance the same amount on two old mahogany wardrobes in the place if they would give me a deed of trust for the latter. This they promised to do. I therefore gave them two hundred dollars upon a bill of sale for the pianos, but when I went for them, was refused admission to the building. After a long argument with the caretaker I departed and got in communication with Mrs. Martin. Telegram after telegram began to pour into my office. No expense was spared in their composition and I was instructed to reply by telegram, sending them collect. She finally admitted that the pianos had already been mortgaged and that she couldn't sell them. Then I threatened arrest and finally Mrs. Martin paid over the money to my lawyer. All of the telegrams sent me in this instance were signed J. H. Baskett, while the only conversation I had with either woman was at the time of the original meeting. All their business was done by telephone or telegraph."

Efforts subsequently were made to sell one of the pianos in question to E. T. Hildebrand, a Roanoke music teacher. Mrs. Martin told him she was about to reopen a school out of money from a "Carnegie Fund" which she was to receive. It was necessary to cancel all old debts of the school before the new funds would become available. The piano was being sold for this purpose. Hildebrand was about to close the deal when he learned the piano had already been sold. In his case, too, fictitious names were used and there were masses of telegrams.

At times the sisters' tactics worked well, as when Colonel Sidney Sheltman of Christiansburg lent them fifteen hundred dollars on the school property, and assumed payment of a mortgage amounting to four thousand dollars. More often, businessmen were first intrigued and later put off by the female negotiators.

One other enigmatic tale about them received wide circulation. At 24 Wells Place N.E., in Roanoke, Mrs. R. E. Hancock related it to newspapermen. She recalled that a year ago on Easter Sunday a four-month-old baby had been left on her rear porch in a basket, a calico garment and gray cloak wrapped around it. Mrs. Hancock and her husband were drawn to the child, christened it Rita Josephine, and made it part of the family.

Within a few weeks, two women wearing black came to stay at their boardinghouse. The older, Mrs. Martin, developed an inordinate fondness for the baby, so much so that the other boarders started calling it the "Martin baby." When little Rita Josephine developed a slight cold, the elderly woman spoke to her for hours on end. She suggested to Mrs. Hancock that she be allowed to take the baby to Christiansburg, where the air was better, the food more healthful. So persistent were her demands that the foster mother almost acceded. When she told her husband, however, he refused.

Mrs. Martin then went to Christiansburg. Her sister remained behind in case the Hancocks should change their mind. Telephone calls from Mrs. Martin now inundated the Roanoke home, all pleading with them to bring the baby to her. Eventually the battle was abandoned. Virginia Wardlaw followed her sister home, leaving behind a room in chaotic disorder, as well as two suitcases. When these were not called for, Mrs. Hancock opened them. In the one she found expensive clothing to provide for the entire first year of a baby girl's life. On the neck of a garment Mrs. Hancock thought she detected a salve she had also found on the abandoned baby's clothing.

In the other bag were various papers, including one with different combinations of names written on it: Martin Snead, Ocey Bessie Snead, Ocey Wardlaw Snead, Bessie Gertrude Snead, and Miss Bessie Gertrude Spindle Martin Snead. A newspaper fragment with a Cincinnati dateline read, "Sustaining the will of Mercy Hail, in which her entire estate of $15,000 is left to her daughter, Anna Hail, noted for her advocacy of putting to painless death the hopelessly sick and fatally hurt." Another, datelined Lockport, New York, read: "Mrs. Edward Skinner died last evening from the effects of a dose of sulphuric acid taken four months ago with suicide intent. The lining of her mouth and throat were badly burned, and she had been unable to take any nourishment. The coroner today issued a certificate of death from starvation."

In small towns, and especially in the South where the oral tradition has always flourished, news travels fast. The accounts from near and far of the three sisters' escapades became the main source of Christiansburg conversations. What was the relation of the Roanoke baby to Mrs. Martin? Was it possibly a child of Ocey Snead's? In town, Bessie Spindle assured people it was not and that she knew of no reason why Ocey and Fletcher should have gone through a second marriage ceremony. Her denial only kindled further speculation. The prolix business negotiations were much remarked upon, as was the insurance on the younger members of the family. The newspaper clippings, with their recurrent theme of violence, seemed almost to foreshadow Ocey Snead's death. The ever spookier happenings at Montgomery College caused increasing consternation. A dread and horror of the women in black developed, with predictable consequences. Life for them became untenable.

At the school the disorder went past endurance as gangs of older boys went on marauding expeditions, trying to see how much damage they could do to the premises. The front door was entirely broken down and knocked to pieces. One group climbed to the roof of the building and tore off the shingles. The latticework on the side was knocked off and stomped upon. On a night sweep, the icehouse in back was left in a shambles and almost every pane of glass in the main building broken. Both young and old students defiantly swung on the lower limbs of the yard's lovely firs and elms, breaking many of the branches.

In the classrooms, relative quiet usually reigned until the morning's ten o'clock recess. After that, disobedience, disorder, and idleness took over. At one point, after a local election, opposing political factions got into a fight which saw some of the boys drawing knives. The girls had been the first to drop out of the school. The boys now followed suit.

Ridicule and abuse were all that remained for the women in black. Every lawyer in town seemed to have some kind of claim against them, every businessman some debt which he was attempting to dun them for. By 1908 the struggle was over. One by one the three sisters left Christiansburg, as did Ocey and Fletcher Snead. Wagging tongues pursued them to New York, where they carried on their multifarious activities designed to recoup the family fortunes. All their efforts were unsuccessful but no word of this ever reached the

South — not, that is, until the desperate machinations were brought to a halt by the death of Ocey Snead, "dear, sweet, lovable little Ocey," as her young aunt Bessie Spindle described her, the "one bright ray" piercing the overshadowing clouds.

13

AS REMARKABLE AS THE EERIE STORIES emanating from the South were the ready explanations for many of them which Franklin Fort was able to provide in New York. Ocey Snead was most certainly the child of Caroline Martin, he said, and there was a birth certificate to prove it. The Hancock child was unrelated, and Mrs. Martin's fondness for it only demonstrated the tender side of her nature.

The sisters had exerted no undue influence on the Snead boys, said Fort. Neither John nor Fletcher had lived happily with his wife for very long. John had been separated from his wife for months before his death. It was true that he had reassigned an insurance policy on his life from her to his Aunt Virginia. He had done so voluntarily, partly because he wished to prevent his wife from realizing on it, and partly because he wanted to express gratitude to his aunt for her help when he was a student. She had paid for his tuition and other expenses. When his wife had sued to have the assignment set aside, Virginia Wardlaw had, in fact, been ill. She was not even a party to the litigation, which eventually achieved a compromise, dividing the insurance money evenly between the two families.

Fletcher Snead was not heavily insured. After his divorce he had sold an insurance policy on his life to one of his wife's brothers, as he did not care to continue carrying it. The brother had bought the policy outright, and no claim was ever made by any member of Fletcher's family for any interest in it. The sisters had likewise laid no claims to his other insurance. Payment would have to await confirmation of his death. Without such confirmation the law required a seven-year waiting period.

As for the two wedding ceremonies between Ocey and Fletcher Snead, the first in Louisville, Kentucky, had taken place in secret because the family, rather than driving them together against their will, had at first opposed the union. When the sisters were later won over, the second ceremony had been performed a month before the birth of the first child, this on January 13, 1908, in Jersey City, New Jersey.

The couple were devoted to one another, Fort stated firmly. As evidence of their affection, he produced yet another document, a tender letter from Ocey to Fletcher after he had left the scene. Written in August 1909, shortly after the birth of the couple's second child, it had never been mailed because Fletcher had left no address.

My Darling Husband,
If you had received a letter every time that I have thought of you, you would indeed have received many, many letters from your "Little Girl," who loves you so dearly. I do so long to see you. Our little baby has arrived. It is a perfectly formed child, not a blemish on it anywhere. Everyone who sees it remarks on its perfections. I will now relieve your suspense of mind and tell you that we have a son. He is the image of you, a lovely intelligent baby boy, and has your hair, eyes, and features. His disposition is sweet and lovely. In this and in every way he is like his dear father. I know he will also be a comfort to you, especially in your old days. He will love you better than anyone else in the whole world.

When he puts his little arm around your neck and nestles against your heart I know you will think of me lovingly for his sake and you will tenderly love him for my sake. When I look at our baby I love you more than ever, if that were possible. Long before our baby came I loved you with all the devotion of which the human heart is capable, but now motherhood has expanded my heart to hold still more love for my precious husband . . .

I trust your health has much improved from the day you went away ill . . . Our Bible, as you know, darling, tells us it is more important to save our own soul than to gain the whole world. And so I pray, my darling, that whatever may betide in this world, you will make sure. of your immortal salvation. And then in Heaven you and I and our two little ones shall be safely gathered in the arms of Jesus. There we shall be forever happy and forever safe from harm.

I vividly remember just before you went away with tears in your eyes you said to me, "Will you always love me no matter what might happen to me?" I tell you now as I told you then, YES, forever and ever, now as then with my fondest kiss for my precious husband. I love you always with all my heart and soul and mind and strength. And so I know you will always truly deeply love

Your adoring
WIFE

The third brother, Albert Snead, also said to be heavily insured, had contacted Fort from his home in Colorado. He had bought a small tract of fruit land in a valley near Palisade. Here he lived alone. The allegations of heavy insurance policies on his life were false, he said, the sum in question amounting to only fifteen hundred dollars, of which his mother, Mary Snead, was the beneficiary. He had not heard from Ocey Snead for months before her death, nor from

Fletcher. He did not know whether the latter was alive or not. He himself did not wish to be drawn into the case, although he did feel strongly about it.

"She ought to be released," he wrote of the incarcerated Virginia Wardlaw. "She is one of the most loving and self-sacrificing women that ever lived. She never had any connection with the death of Ocey Snead."

To further counter disclosures from the South, Fort had written to friends of Virginia Wardlaw in that section. She herself had refused to give him any names, he said, not wanting them connected with hers while she was under charges so infamous. He had been forced to go to family friends in the North. The lawyer's letter spoke of the "utterly and despicably groundless charge of murder made without even a decent basis of suspicion," and said this charge was being strongly pushed by the press and some of the public authorities who had worked themselves into a hysterical condition, unprecedented in his view.

"Every circumstance of her life, upon which her natural pride and reticence have refused information, has been treated as though it were the covering of a disgraceful scandal and insinuation, and brutal deduction has followed, until a Northerner such as I am is ashamed of the utter lack of decency, chivalry, and concern for a defenseless woman," Fort wrote. "May I ask you to add your tribute to the character of Virginia Wardlaw? Every statement herein made comes from a sincere and utter confidence in her innocence and the loftiest admiration for her beautiful and wonderful character."

From William R. Webb, headmaster of the Webb School for Boys in Buckletree, Tennessee, came an early reply. Saying he had known the prisoner for long years, he described her as "mysterious in not taking people into her confidence, in not mixing with people," but a woman of high character.

"She would not have committed murder," said Webb, "even
if she is proud and sensitive."

Virginia Wardlaw's brother-in-law, Richard Spindle,
wrote from Christiansburg that family resources were sufficient to help meet defense needs; while relations had not
been intimate recently, he would do what was necessary.

14

WHEREAS THE YOUNG LAWYER was ever more firmly convinced of his client's innocence, the prosecution, notwith-
standing his efforts, was equally certain of her guilt. At her
first appearance in court Virginia Wardlaw had been arraigned for murder. A second hearing had been scheduled to
determine if she should be released on bail pending action
by the grand jury. This second hearing, scheduled for Monday, December 6, was postponed until the following Saturday. As in all such cases, there were to be no witnesses for
the prisoner.

Before the actual engagement in court, there was continued press sparring between the two sides, the sort of grand-
standing which has often brought American criminal court
procedures into disrepute. Principally at issue were the matters of the genuineness of the suicide note and the twenty-
four-hour period which intervened between Ocey Snead's
death and her aunt's call to the police. It was believed that
Franklin Fort would try to show his client had spent Sunday
night with her sisters at 466 West 22nd Street, Manhattan;
that she only came back to East Orange on Monday afternoon and called the police right after finding the body. Occupants of 466 had been questioned, however, and to their

knowledge she had not come there on Sunday night. To reporters, Fort maintained that the twenty-four-hour interval could be explained, that it was in any event less crucial than the suicide note. "The entire case against Virginia Wardlaw rests on the question of whether the note was written by her or is a forgery," he insisted. "Ocey Snead either wrote it herself without the knowledge of anyone, or it is a forgery. The talk that she may have been forced to write it is absurd."

Police Chief James Bell asserted he had at least a dozen specimens of the dead girl's handwriting, not one of which corresponded completely with the suicide note. Experts had been called in and at least one would testify at the hearing. It was true, the chief admitted, that on first glance the handwriting of all the principal members of the family was similar in many respects. As for the twenty-four-hour waiting period, Bell said that to him it remained a mystery.

At half past eight on Saturday morning, December 11, Virginia Wardlaw was again driven to the City Hall at East Orange. The hearing began in the council chamber shortly after nine o'clock, with many of the case's principals present. The Essex County prosecutor, Wilbur Mott, peered over his glasses and looked as stern as his office demanded; Police Chief Bell appeared appropriately broad-shouldered and authoritative; while the middle-aged county recorder, Francis A. Nott, Jr., looked like the typical well-kempt court official. From Nott would come the decision as to whether the prisoner should be held for the grand jury or released. For the defense, Franklin Fort made a debonair impression, sporting a stylish derby on arrival. The main focus of all eyes, however, was Virginia Wardlaw. Hiding behind newspapers, she followed her counsel into the courtroom, taking her place near the railing. As usual, she was clad in black and swathed in veils. One, a gauzy fabric, closely fitted her countenance; another spread out like a curtain from the rim of a large, wide hat; still another, of heavier material, fell down her back. The black, cloaklike garments she wore seemed also to be multiple, broadening her shoulders, billowing out from the waist. An air of hauteur, of authority and pride seemed to emanate from her figure.

In an opening statement, Prosecutor Mott said he would show that the prisoner's conduct pointed unerringly to her guilt, that she had either induced her niece by hypnotic suggestion to commit suicide, or actually led her to a violent death by placing her body in the bathtub. Assailing her habits of life, he maintained they were not in keeping with those of the ultrarefined South from which she came. Countering, Franklin Fort insisted the state would not be able to prove either the commission of a crime or a motive. The forgery note was genuine, he said; Ocey Snead a suicide. His client, as a matter of simple justice, should be released.

While these opponents spoke, Virginia Wardlaw rearranged her veils in a businesslike way and began taking notes. Writing in a clear hand, her short pencil moved rapidly and precisely over a quire of yellow legal foolscap. Sometimes she would lift her pencil nervously in the air, then let her hand pounce down on the paper as if she had caught some point in her favor. Counting the value of each word, she appeared more like an interested but somewhat detached observer than a prisoner accused of murder.

The voluminous note-taking continued as the state began its parade of twelve witnesses with Sergeant Timothy Caniff of the East Orange police force. He told of receiving the prisoner's call at 4:40 P.M. on Monday, November 29, reporting "an accident." The accident, he learned, was a death in the house. In response to the request for a coroner, he had sent Deputy County Physician Herbert Simmons, who later told him the case warranted an investigation.

Dr. Simmons, a handsome young man with a neatly

trimmed mustache, took the stand. He described his discovery of the body of Ocey Snead. The head, he said, was almost directly under the faucet, the nostrils and mouth completely immersed, one hand partially closed and loosely grasping a washrag. Nearby, a note was pinned to some clothes. His examination showed the victim to have been dead about twenty-four hours. When Virginia Wardlaw gave no adequate explanation for not reporting the matter earlier, Dr. Simmons called the police station and recommended an investigation. He placed this call at 5:15 P.M.

Sergeant William O'Neill — round-faced, hair parted in the middle in turn of the century style — told of being met at the door by an aged woman and led through the dark house, of finding the dead body. With difficult prodding, O'Neill had gained meager details about the victim — her name, the fact that her husband and first child were dead, a second in the hospital. She had lived in the house about ten days, the woman said. When he called attention to the fact that the suicide note was written in pen and ink, he asked where they might be. Virginia Wardlaw told him she did not know; a search of the house later turned up neither pen nor ink. Remnants of food were found, and the one cot for sleeping.

"The last time she had seen Mrs. Snead alive was on the afternoon of the previous day," O'Neill testified on a crucial point. "She had not been to the bathroom in the twenty-four hours before discovering the body. Miss Wardlaw said that she had not been upstairs at all since Mrs. Snead left her on Saturday saying that she was going to take a bath and a long sleep. She said that she was in the house all the time that intervened except for an hour, when she went out to do a little shopping."

Civic pride came to the fore when Prosecutor Mott asked Chief James Bell to take the stand, describing him as "the beautiful chief of the beautiful city of East Orange." The

beautiful chief did little more than confirm previous findings.

Undertaker Gustave Kunz told the court that no member
of the family had claimed or visited the body of Ocey Snead
while it rested in his care. "When a person with mother and
other close relatives living, dies, and the body lies on view
for more than a week and neither the mother nor any of the
relatives come to see it, it is a most suspicious circumstance,"
Prosecutor Mott interjected. Kunz concluded by describing
the burial at Mount Hope, where only the victim's aunt,
Mary Snead, represented the family.

Detective Alfred J. Harding testified to his search of the
East Orange house. In the cellar he had found a package
wrapped in a newspaper dated Sunday, November 28. Two
other detectives told of the bare condition of the House of
Mystery in Brooklyn.

When Dr. William McKenzie described the dissection of
Ocey Snead's body during the autopsy, Virginia Wardlaw's
shoulders moved convulsively. Some thought she was sobbing but in actuality she was accelerating her vigorous note-
taking. Earlier, Dr. McKenzie had expressed the view that
Ocey Snead was murdered. In court, he was more
restrained. "Water in the lungs entered when the woman
was alive. She was alive when she got into the tub," the physician declared, "but whether in her weakened condition her
head was held under the water until she was drowned or
whether she was unconscious when put into the tub I cannot
say." The small amount of water which had entered apparently made any definitive conclusion impossible. Stitches
from an operation performed months before were still present at death, Dr. McKenzie added.

The first real excitement of the hearing came with the appearance of William J. Kinsley, a handwriting expert, introduced by Mott as having handled 964 cases of questioned

documents. "In my opinion, the pen used for the signature 'Ocey W. M. Snead' is not the pen used to sign the body of the note," Kinsley told an attentive court. "The person who wrote the note held the pen obliquely — off from the right shoulder so to speak. In the body of the note the letters are close together and the shading is on the upstroke. In the signature the 'O' and the 'W' are somewhat the same. But in the word 'Snead' the letters are far apart and the shading is on the downstroke. The body was written with a heavy stub and the signature with a fine one."

"Do you believe the note was written long before the time it was found?" Prosecutor Mott asked.

"I am not entirely able to say. There is a slight tear, a slanting one, on the upper surface of the paper, taking a part off one of the letters, and showing that the tear was made after the note was written. If it had been otherwise, the ink would have traveled over the paper after the tear. This tear may prove some sign of age to the document."

"Have you compared any known standards of Ocey Snead's handwriting with the suicide note?"

"I have seen two signatures of Ocey Snead that I have been told were actually hers."

"Have you formed an opinion from them whether it was she who wrote the suicide note?"

"I have not."

The two signatures furnished Kinsley were from Brooklyn lawyer Julius Carabba. When at the Flatlands House of Mystery, Carabba had given Ocey Snead a check which she endorsed, but later complained she could not get cashed. Carabba had then given her five dollars, for which she had signed a receipt. The check, endorsed in ink, and the receipt, in pencil, were both written while Ocey Snead was lying in bed, hence poor specimens.

When Prosecutor Mott stated his belief that the use of two

pens, probably well in advance of death, suggested premedi-
tated murder, Franklin Fort protested strongly. The use of
several pens and perhaps different inks proved, rather, that
Ocey Snead had contemplated suicide for a long time, he
said. If this was the case, it also accounted for the fact that
no pen or ink was found in the house.

Dr. Charles E. Teeter, of Roseville, recounted from the
stand his unusual late-night call on Ocey Snead. "I didn't
feel like going, and tried to beg off, but she insisted," he
said, referring to Virginia Wardlaw. "She drove me in a cab
to a house on North Fourteenth Street and took me upstairs,
where a young woman was lying on a cot, partly dressed
and partly covered with bedclothes. There was no heat in
the house and I asked the reason why, as the weather was
cold. The older woman told me the furnace was out of repair, but that she had a fire in the kitchen for cooking. The
patient appeared to be anemic, but a hurried examination
satisfied me she was not ill beyond a slight trace of bronchitis. I filled out the certificate of health which had been requested. No more conversation occurred until I left the
house, when this older woman asked me what time it was. I
told her it was ten thirty. She paid my fee and I left. On
several subsequent occasions, when I was asked to call at the
house to attend to the young woman, Miss Wardlaw said
that I needn't be concerned about my fee, as the young lady
was insured for a large amount of money."

Dr. William Pettit, the last witness called, proved to be
troublesome to both prosecution and defense, insisting on
reiterating opinions which had no bearing on the case. With
difficulty Prosecutor Mott led him through key passages, beginning with a description of the House of Mystery in
Brooklyn.

"The blinds were always drawn down," he recalled. "Once
I raised one of them on a bright day, but Miss Wardlaw

lowered it. Barring one or two times, I never saw anything to eat in the house. Miss Wardlaw was always present. The sick woman was seldom able to answer any of my questions. Miss Wardlaw or one of the other women who were present would always answer for her. Miss Wardlaw took notes on various occasions when I was present of what I said or did."

"This sick girl, what was her state?" asked Prosecutor Mott. "Was she unconscious?"

"Not exactly. Subconscious, I should say."

"What do you mean by subconscious?"

"Well, as if she were in a state of hypnosis."

"Did you ever find any drugs or stimulants in the house?"

"On one occasion I saw a bottle of chloroform. I asked the defendant what it was for and she said that she thought I might need it. I said I would bring choloroform with me when I needed it."

Several weeks after the birth of Ocey Snead's baby, Dr. Pettit related, he performed an operation on the mother. Several times thereafter he called to remove the stitches, but was told by Miss Wardlaw that she wanted to have them left on for a few days, as the patient was very weak. Dr. Pettit found it harder and harder to see his patient, and on one occasion entered through a window when the front door was locked.

When he insisted on payment, Virginia Wardlaw at one time gave him five dollars, another time a note for one hundred. "This surprised me," Dr. Pettit testified, "as my bill was not that amount. I thought it worthless and refused it. Then Miss Wardlaw showed me a will of the young woman, bequeathing most of her personal and real property to her grandmother and giving me a thousand dollars for my services and kindnesses, payable at her death. The young woman might not live long, she told me. I refused to accept it. I was disgusted and thought the situation so suspicious that I re-

ported it to a former Brooklyn police captain named Reyn-
olds. I don't believe anything was ever done, however."

On cross-examination, Fort asked Dr. Pettit about his
technical training. The Brooklyn physician conceded that his
knowledge of hypnosis was slight, that he did not use it in
his own practice. As for the choloroform, Fort made him
admit it was not unusual to have this soporific fluid on hand
in emergencies, such as the period when a child is born.
Even the identity of Virginia Wardlaw was called into question. After hearing of the similarities in dress and physiog-
nomy of the three sisters, Dr. Pettit acknowledged he could
not always be sure which sister he was referring to at any
given time.

Summing up the case presented by the prosecution's
lineup of witnesses, Fort asked for a dismissal of the complaint against his client. "There is not the slightest suggestion of proof that death resulted from violent means," he
emphasized. "The state has a note in evidence but there has
been no proof nor even a hint of proof that the note was not
written by Ocey Snead. A handwriting expert has been introduced but he is unable to say that the note was a forgery.
The hypnotism evidence introduced by Dr. Pettit is a farce,
since he admits he knows practically nothing about hypnosis, has had little experience with it. It seems to me that a
condition of hysteria has prevailed among the public and the
authorities in the conduct of this case. Things seemingly 'peculiar' have been discovered as to my client but the prosecution as the result of two weeks of effort has failed to produce
anything even dishonorable as to her character, her motives,
or her acts. The evidence submitted has consisted of vague
insinuations of crime. Until the state comes before you with
some proof of the definite guilt of Virginia Wardlaw, you
have no basis on which to hold her. I demand her release."

"If she is adjudged innocent, it will be the most remark-

*The East Orange house where Ocey Snead met her death
in a four-foot bathtub.*

A pensive look characterizes this best-known likeness of Ocey Snead, the bathtub victim.

*Fletcher Snead, who left his wife under mysterious circumstances,
never to return.*

Last year my little daughter died. Other near and dear ones have gone before. I want to join them in Heaven. I have been prostrated with illness a long time. When you read this I I will have committed suicide. Do not grieve for me. Rejoice with me that Death brings me a blessed relief from pain and suffering greater than I can bear.

@W. M. Snead.

The original suicide note found near the body of Ocey Snead.

My little daughter has died. Other near and dear ones have died. I want to join them in Heaven. I have been prostrated with illness a long time. When you have read this I will be dead from suicide. Do not grieve for me. Rejoice with me that death brings me a painless sleep, blessed relief from sickness suffering and pain greater than I can bear.

Ocey W. M. Snead

Last year my little daughter died. Other near and dear kindred too have gone to Heaven. I long to go there too. I have been very weak and ill a long time. Death well be a blessed relief to me in my suffering. When you read this I will have committed suicide. My sorrow and pain in this world are greater than I can endure.

Ocey W. M. Snead.

Two of a number of additional suicide notes found in Mrs. Martin's possession at the Bayard Hotel.

A History of Rutherford County

The public square in Murfreesboro, Tennessee, about 1910. When the sisters lived there only five years earlier it was much the same, save perhaps for the presence of the automobile.

Newark Evening News

Montgomery College in Christiansburg, Virginia, where the three sisters taught until sinister whisperings drove them from the scene.

Lawyer Franklin Fort and
Virginia Wardlaw.

Prosecutor Wilbur Mott.

Dr. Herbert Simmons.

Reverend Albert Wardlaw.

"BATHTUB TRAGEDY" CASE

New York World

Sergeant William O'Neill.

Handwriting expert
William Kinsley.

Mrs. Bessie Spindle.

Albert Snead.

Newark Evening Star

Virginia Wardlaw on one of her last journeys to court. The stern face betrayed little of the beauty that was once hers (see inset).

New York World

An artist for the New York World rendered this impression of the redoubtable Mrs. Martin, eldest of the three sisters and mother of Ocey Snead. (Inset) Mary Snead, the most retiring member of the trio.

able case of a person having been a victim of circumstances that has ever come under the observation of the prosecutor," Wilbur Mott summed up his side of the argument. "Innocent persons do not maintain such a silence in the face of a charge involving their very lives when explanations which they could make might clear up the whole matter. I have waited for two weeks for an explanation of some circumstances which are certainly suspicious in this case. None has been forthcoming."

After a brief review of the testimony, Recorder Nott ordered the prisoner held without bail for action of the Essex County grand jury, the legal requirement of probable cause having been met to his satisfaction. His decision, he said, was based on two main points. First, the prisoner had remained downstairs in a bleak house for almost twenty-four hours after the death of Ocey Snead, never once visiting the upper floor or seeking to ascertain the condition of the ailing girl. Her explanations for this peculiar behavior were unsatisfactory. Secondly, the evidence appeared conclusive that the pen which signed the suicide note was not the same one that wrote the rest of the document. This circumstance, together with the likelihood the note had been written some time ago, cast a further suspicion of foul play.

"Too rotten for comment," was Franklin Fort's reaction to the decision.

"How quickly can you transcribe that evidence?" Virginia Wardlaw asked him an instant later. With the utmost composure she rolled up the notes she herself had taken, raised a newspaper to her face, and left the room on the arm of her attorney. Outside, entering the carriage which was to take her back to the jail cell in Newark, she appeared unmoved by the decision.

Three days later William S. Gummere, New Jersey's chief

justice, charged the December grand jury and placed the case in their hands with these words: "On November 29, last, Ocey Snead was found in a bathtub in East Orange and at the time of her death she and her aunt, Miss Wardlaw, were the only inmates of the house. Whether the girl died voluntarily or at the hands of another is a matter which you ought to determine by your investigation. That she did not die a natural death has been practically determined.

"One of the officers who visited the house immediately after the authorities were notified by Miss Wardlaw found, among other things, a note purporting to have been written by the Snead woman in which she said she was about to commit suicide. If she wrote the note, it is quite fair to assume that death was the result of her own act. If she did not, it is to be presumed that her death was the act of another. In investigating this matter it is your function to hear all the evidence, to weigh all the evidence and determine whether any particular crime has been committed and whether probable grounds of guilt are shown. If the evidence presented to you by the state causes you to deem it probable that some person committed murder, then it is your duty to indict. Otherwise you must refuse to indict. You will find the case a very mysterious one. It is important that you give it all the time and all the care and scrutiny which it deserves."

15

WITH ONE SISTER BEHIND BARS awaiting grand jury action and a second under surveillance in Manhattan, police intensified their search for the third, the elusive Mrs. Martin.

Why did that enigmatic figure remain in hiding rather than come to the defense of her sister? Was her continued retreat an implication of guilt? Where was she?

Persistent rumors said that Mrs. Martin had been seen recently in Roanoke and Christiansburg. One said she was hiding in the Montgomery College building, protected by caretaker Floyd Haden who, armed with a gun, had declared he would kill the first man to enter without a written permit. When these rumors were checked, it was learned the eldest sister had last been in the South in October and early November, working on the intricate type of business negotiations which was her specialty. Haden had not seen her, although he wished he had. No paycheck had reached him in months and he wished to turn the school keys over to the proper authority. In her travels Mrs. Martin had followed her custom of bypassing the depot's ticket window and paying her fare on the train. As usual, no one knew where she was going. In New York, however, a variety of clues made police certain she was in their midst. Tracing her movements over the years they turned up a life portrait to stagger the imagination of a fiction writer.

An index card at the office of New York's Board of Education provided the first strokes: "Mrs. Caroline B. W. Martin, née Wardlaw, appointed Jan. 6, 1868, — came back May 1, 1871 and was appointed principal of the Girls' Grammar School, No. 17, at 335 West 47th Street, June 3, 1896. Retired Sept. 1, 1902."

Also on file was the report on a meeting of the board on May 28, 1902: "The Committee on Elementary Schools reports that it has under consideration an application for retirement from Mrs. C. B. W. Martin, principal of Public School No. 17 in Manhattan. The City Superintendent reports that he considers Mrs. Martin mentally incapacitated for the position of principal of a public school, and recommends that she be retired, to take effect Sept. 1, 1901. After considering all facts in the case, your committee is of the opinion that the best interests of the school system would be subserved by the retirement of Mrs. Martin. It concurs in the recommendation of the Superintendent of Schools. Retired accordingly following section 1092 of the charter, annuity fixed at $1,000 annually, one-half her salary at date of retirement."

Police were able to contact John Jasper, superintendent of schools at the time of Mrs. Martin's retirement, who acknowledged he was responsible for that action. "There were some who thought I acted with haste but I think time has proved it otherwise," he said. "Mrs. Martin was dismissed for incompetency. She had a strong pull, maybe because she was a charming conversationalist, an accomplished letter writer, and generally speaking a very shrewd woman."

Miss E. Richards, secretary to Jasper, remembered well the visits of Mrs. Martin to his office, usually relating to some difficulty with school officials. She was often accompanied by her daughter Ocey. In Miss Richards's view, the result of many conversations, the mother was a woman of compelling appearance, superior education, and remarkable business ability.

Miss Mary Byrne, who taught at Public School number 17 while Mrs. Martin was its principal, recalled that her superior was always having differences with creditors, many of whom called at the school. This was one of a number of reasons why Miss Byrne felt that the principal, although intellectually brilliant, was not taking good care of the school.

No one seemed to question that Mrs. Martin was gifted; likewise no one failed to note her peculiarities. Mrs. Elizabeth Ackerman of 302 West 47th Street had been a pupil at number 17 while her father, Joseph, was the school's long-time janitor. She recalled Mrs. Martin's habit of collecting newspapers and other periodicals, which were found littered about her office. On several occasions Mrs. Martin had asked to use the janitor's home as a mail drop, although she had the school address and a residence of her own. "Mrs. Martin was regarded as a remarkably brainy woman," Mrs. Ackerman commented, "yet she possessed characteristics that aroused critics."

Mrs. Martha K. Harkness, of 318 West 47th Street, assistant principal of the school from 1896 to 1902, had a like view of the many-sided Mrs. Martin, whom she characterized as "shrewd and foreseeing," but also as "a woman of many peculiarities" and "an unspeakable woman, who treated both teachers and pupils abominably." Her first recollection was of an event which occurred shortly after Mrs. Martin was made principal.

"She called me in one day and asked me to loan her eighty-five dollars and fifty cents," Mrs. Harkness recounted. "I told her I couldn't let her have the money, whereupon she tried to hypnotize me. She looked me very sharp in the eyes and kept repeating, 'You'll loan me that money!' She didn't get me, though, and I went home. After telling her several times she was mistaken because I would not let her have the money, she stopped asking me. From then on, however, I kept being bothered to death with tradesmen calling at my home trying to collect bills against Mrs. Martin. They simply visited me to find out where she lived. She kept moving about from place to place so often, though, that I could not help them."

Mrs. Harkness also spoke of other queer occurrences. "One I remember in particular," she said. "Dr. O'Brien, who was one of our superintendents, came to visit the school when Mrs. Martin was not in the office. I sent for her and she sent back word that she would be down in a minute. Dr.

O'Brien waited for a long time and then we found that Mrs. Martin had left the school by a back door.

"Once, Mrs. Martin fell on the sidewalk in front of the Vanderbilt home at Fifth and 58th Street. She had been badly hurt and brought suit against the Vanderbilts. While this was pending, she appeared about the school on crutches all the time. I don't think she got any money, however, or else she did, for it wasn't long before she completely abandoned her crutches."

Police were particularly intrigued to learn that Mrs. Martin always used a stub pen, for handwriting expert Kinsley had said part of Ocey Snead's suicide note appeared to have been written with such a tool. "I remember very well that Mrs. Martin always used a stub pen, no matter how little writing she may have had to do," Mrs. Harkness stated. "She had difficulty in getting pens to suit her, and I am under the impression she had them made to order. But I remember very well that she was a crank on the subject of stub pens."

From Mrs. Ackerman police learned that Mrs. Martin had had a second child, a little son, in addition to her daughter Ocey. The boy, said Mrs. Ackerman, appeared to be sadly mistreated. Mrs. Harkness confirmed this impression in grim terms.

"Her treatment of her little son, Hugh Martin, was exceptionally noticeable to us all," she said. "The little fellow, one of the brightest and dearest chaps I've ever known, attended school where his mother taught before she was principal. Later, when she came here, she had a hot lunch served to her, but all the child got for his lunches were a few crackers and cakes or other odds and ends given him by the other teachers from their luncheons. Nor would his mother allow him to walk anywhere but behind her. Ocey had to do the same thing. Whenever she was out with her mother, she too had to walk behind. In the fall of 1888, Hugh was stricken with spinal meningitis and died."

From other former pupils and teachers, police heard that the first Martin child had fallen down a long flight of stairs, with injuries that proved fatal. A death certificate was found which revealed that Hugh Martin was born in 1881 at 37 East 39th Street, Manhattan, the same fashionable address where his sister Ocey was born four years later. Death came on November 30, 1888, at the age of seven years and three months, the cause listed as spinal meningitis, plus convulsions and exhaustion. The father, Colonel Martin, was sixty years old at the time, while Caroline Martin, the mother, was a much younger forty-two.

The accounts of little Hugh's death, with its pattern of deprivation, illness, and untimely accident so reminiscent of other family tragedies, were soon matched in police files by the melodramatic events of the father's life.

Born into a distinguished Southern family, Robert Maxwell Martin was thirty-three years old when the Civil War broke out. He enlisted as an officer, swiftly reached the rank of colonel, and became one of the most dashing soldiers of the Confederacy. On one occasion he was credited with saving the life of General John Hunt Morgan, the hero of many daring raids against the North. After serving as one of Morgan's men, Colonel Martin succeeded to the command of the Third Kentucky Cavalry. Along with another officer, he became the author of an audacious plot to abduct Vice President-elect Andrew Johnson. Johnson was scheduled to go through Louisville, Kentucky, by stage on his way to the inauguration. By an accidental change of plans the passage through the city was made by boat. The prize thus escaped the plotters.

After the war, Colonel Martin settled in Louisville, where he became the center of much controversy over his refusal ever to sign an oath of allegiance to the United States. He entered the tobacco industry, succeeding through his wide knowledge of the business and his knack for choosing the right speculation. Some of his income went into a house in Wilder Park, a spacious suburb of Louisville.

The time had now come for the retired war hero to marry. The bride he chose was an attractive young woman from a well-known Southern family. Caroline Wardlaw had just returned from a trip abroad. In addition to being comely, she was gifted with a cultivated, resourceful mind. It was true that she was a good deal younger than the colonel. This did not worry him, although perhaps it should have. The young bride wrote a letter which East Orange police unearthed in one of the many suitcases in their possession. It indicated that her motives for marriage were not entirely pure. Addressed to *My own darling mother*, it began as follows:

You have been so good to me in the way of letters, as well as all your life in other things, that I find myself so deeply in debt to you I hardly know how to begin to answer all your precious letters. I know how closely occupied you are, and how you strive oft-times in great weariness of flesh and spirit, so I appreciate still more deeply your love and care in writing to me. May God make me in all things a dutiful daughter and grant that I may have the joy of spending the remainder of my life at your side, ministering to your comfort and joining in the unbroken circle of your children under one and the same roof, in a family home whence we shall go no more out in separation until one by one leave earth for the home in heaven to which the Saviour's blood gives us access and title. Through all trials, you both, as well as every sister and brother, I love with a consuming passionate love. My marriage undertaken to advance my opportu-

nities for helping you all, my precious ones, has not in the slightest degree diminished this deep, immortal love for you . . .

After going on to other family matters, the letter concluded with more endearments and the signature "Carrie."

For Colonel Martin, married life was not what he had expected. He had met his young wife on her return from a trip. She was indeed a traveler, not only to Europe but more frequently to New York, or to visit her sisters in the South. She also took a great interest in business, being as fascinated by speculation as he. Her ventures were not always profitable.

One night, mysteriously, the Wilder Park mansion burned to the ground. Queer rumors circulated in the neighborhood when it was learned it had been insured for twenty-two thousand dollars. Although the origins of the blaze were never ascertained, the insurance was paid in full.

The colonel had made one quick fortune and lost it just as rapidly. Now he and his wife moved to New York, where he established himself in the tobacco field he knew and made another. His wife set up a private school, then shifted to public school teaching. A son, Hugh, and a daughter, Ocey, were born. The Martins lived in fashionable Murray Hill on East 39th Street. Once again life was good.

But not for long. Tragedy struck the life of little Hugh. The colonel met a new series of business reverses and finally went home alone to Louisville, to live in a smaller house built on the site of the old mansion.

It was the year 1900 when Mrs. Martin's letters began emphasizing the difficulties she was having with her teaching career. His spirits, too, were down, his grip on life weakening. Once more he made the trip to New York. It was not a good move. His wife appeared distracted, worried about finances. Unaccountably they moved from boardinghouse to boardinghouse. And then, while living in two rooms at 349 West 58th Street, in a rundown house that yet carried echoes of faded Victorian elegance, the colonel suffered a stroke.

Neighbors were disturbed by the relationship between the couple, and by the woman's attitude toward young Ocey who had come to join them. One night a man named Kiefe, who lived in the next room, heard a loud crash, followed by what sounded like groans. When he went next door to knock, there was no reply. The groans continued, joined by the sound of sobbing. Kiefe put his shoulder to the door, broke in, and came upon what he described to police as a frightening and distressing scene. Stretched on the floor, Colonel Martin lay semiconscious and groaning. His wife, half dressed, was lounging on the bed, apparently in a state of complete detachment. In the corner, Ocey stood weeping hysterically.

While Kiefe gazed on the strange scene, Mrs. Martin raised herself on one elbow and looked him firmly in the eye. Then she turned to her daughter with threatening words, "Ocey, remember!" At this, the girl's face took on a dazed expression. She cowered deeper into the corner and became silent. The neighbor took note of the disorder in the room, the soiled clothes and bits of molding food lying about, and hurried out to call a physician. Hours later, the old war hero was dead.

A death certificate gave the date as January 9, 1901, the cause of death as hemiplegia, chronic cystitis, and coma. Burial occurred in Mount Hope Cemetery on January 17. Mrs. Martin paid the first installment on the lot, but when she defaulted on subsequent payments, the body was disinterred and placed in the Confederate burial ground there, the expense to be borne by a group of Southern war veterans. Later it was learned that Colonel Martin was insured for twenty thousand dollars. Caroline Martin, the beneficiary, was approached. She had collected on the policy, but refused to resume payments to the cemetery. She was now officially a widow, although for long years she had worn only widow's black and allowed to go uncorrected the general assumption that her husband was dead.

From all sides came confirmation of Mrs. Martin's erratic behavior and her preoccupation with the dollar. Records of New York's surrogate's court indicated that in 1901 she was appointed guardian of her daughter's estate, the total amounting to twenty-five hundred dollars and consisting of United States two per cent bonds. Two years later, Surrogate Thomas signed an order authorizing her to spend five hundred dollars of this estate for Ocey Snead's school expenses — tuition, food, and other necessaries. On four other occasions, Mrs. Martin petitioned the court for five hundred dollars, each time saying that her daughter was "fitting herself to become a teacher," and that she, the mother, did not have any funds to spare for the education expenses.

Lawyer Maxwell Hall Elliott, with offices at 277 Broadway, told authorities the former schoolteacher had first come to him to borrow on her thousand-dollar annual pension. As a result of her borrowing, Elliott was to receive the pension for some time to come. On her visits, Mrs. Martin always wore black and was heavily veiled, her most striking feature her "staring, almost hypnotic eyes."

"Money was her one idea," said Elliott. "She continually talked about it. She borrowed money of me every six months on her pension and it looks to me as if she had been paying those insurance premiums with this money. Once she said to me, 'If you will let me have a thousand down I will give you my pension for the rest of my life.' Again, she talked incoherently about policies, loans, and once asked me if I would invest five thousand dollars if I could make five hundred per cent. I told her that was too much to make honestly. She would come to this office at nine o'clock in the morning and sit until four in the afternoon talking to me or the secretaries about money matters. She was a kind of mastermind. Once she came here with her sister, Miss Wardlaw, and she had the sister completely under her domination."

A certain incongruity derived from the information supplied by R. B. Smith, treasurer of the Teacher's Mutual Benefit Association. In late 1908, at the very time when Mrs. Martin was known to have sought loans on life insurance policies and real estate, she had neglected to present or cash her pension checks. Because the teacher's association liked to keep its records up-to-date, Smith had written asking her to use them at once. The backlog of checks was then cashed.

Similarly, Mrs. Martin appeared to have a cavalier attitude toward money in the story told by Mrs. William Jones of 262 East 28th Street, one of the many addresses occupied by the clan before its move to Brooklyn's House of Mystery. Mrs. Jones recalled the one circumstance she thought particularly strange. Mrs. Martin repeatedly urged Mrs. Jones's daughter Esther to go to her school in the South. Everything would be free of charge, she said. When the daugher refused, the generous offer was withdrawn and Mrs. Martin lost all interest in Miss Esther.

At an earlier family address, 249 West 48th Street, Manhattan, William Doscher, the landlord, said his most striking memory was of the mother's seeming harshness with her daughter, at that time in her middle teens. "We became greatly attached to Ocey," he related. "Mrs. Martin was frequently cruel to the child, who would come running to my wife and fling her arms around her neck and sob. My wife tried many times to learn what troubled the child, but she would never tell her and we did not discover the nature of the fear she had for her parent. After they had stayed for about seven months without paying us a cent of the rent, we were forced to begin processes to evict them and after a time we were successful. I observed while they were with us that Mrs. Martin seemed to have good standing with prominent people, or at least people who appeared to be of some consequence. She had many callers from among folks of what you would call the upper classes. The stories I have read in the papers about the queer ways of the family agree perfectly with our experience of the mother and child at our house. They were untidy and their rooms were always in the utmost disorder."

"Ocey was the sweetest girl I ever knew," Mrs. Doscher added to her husband's account. "I grew to be very fond of her in the seven months they lived here and she would come softly downstairs to my flat when her mother was out and sometimes throw her arms around my neck and, crying softly, tell me she loved me. She seemed afraid of her mother. Sometimes she brought a message from her mother to me. In delivering it, she would gaze off into space and repeat the message like a lesson in a dull monotone."

Mrs. Martha Harkness, the assistant principal of Public School number 17, also had a recollection of Ocey Snead that added to the previous picture. Ocey had attended the school before her mother became principal, she said, and seemed as bright and cheerful as any other normal child. "When she was about sixteen she suddenly changed," recalled Mrs. Harkness. "She seemed to draw within herself. She never smiled then. She never laughed like other girls, and seemed morose. A faraway expression came into her face and she acted to me like a child who had learned something that caused a great sorrow to hang over her."

It was when Ocey was at the age of sixteen, authorities already knew, that her father met his death. It was far too late now to look into the circumstances, or to make an investigation of the death of seven-year-old Hugh Martin, Ocey's older brother. Time had obscured too many of the facts which would have to be checked. Not so with the death of Ocey Snead herself. It had occurred only a fortnight ago. And more and more authorities saw Ocey's mother emerging as the dominant figure in the family, as that destiny-tossed clan's complicated Svengali. So far, despite the intense search and publicity, she had eluded their grasp, although several times, at Manhattan hotels and Long Island locations, they appeared to be only a step behind her.

16

AT TWELVE THIRTY ON TUESDAY AFTERNOON, December 14, the telephone rang at Manhattan's Bayard Hotel. Behind the desk, Manager J. L. Woodman picked up the receiver. A woman's voice, with a Southern accent, asked if a room was available. If so, she would be arriving in about a half hour, coming from the Hotel Aldine on Fourth Avenue.

At one o'clock Woodman saw a red cab pull up to 142 West 49th Street. A stout woman got out, encased in black from a wide-brimmed hat down to the bottom of her skirts, which trailed on the ground. Veils shielded her face. Carrying a small black box, she walked slowly up to the desk, moving with the infirmity of age.

"I am very lame and am suffering from nervous indigestion," she said. "My arm is sore. Please register for me. I am Mrs. Maybrick of this city."

Woodward assigned her room 855. The woman paid the

dollar-fifty daily rate with a five dollar bill and asked for writing paper. When the bellboy offered to carry her luggage, she waved him away, saying, "It's got money in it and I'll take care of it myself."

Once ensconced in her room, the woman began to draw attention by her odd behavior. No one was allowed into her room. She ordered a luncheon of chicken broth and buttered toast, but took it from the maid at the door. She ordered every newspaper available from the bellboy, sending him out several times to get the latest editions. She also gave him bulky letters to mail, insisting that he post them outside, on no account in the hotel. At the door to her room, she had opened her little black box to pay him. Inside he saw bank notes and silver.

At four o'clock, the occupant of room 855 asked for a cab and descended. She sat in the lobby while waiting, her spectral presence noted by all who passed. The taxi driver who took her fare also brought her back at six o'clock. When she had returned to her room, he told manager Woodman he had driven her to the Hotel Collingwood, at 45 West 35th Street. She had gone inside, then returned to the cab. For the better part of an hour they had driven aimlessly about the city before coming back to the Bayard.

At this point Woodman called the police. Detectives James Foyle, William O'Grady, and James Stapleton of the New York force arrived. From the account given they were satisfied that the woman was the sought-after Caroline Martin. They informed East Orange. On Wednesday morning, Detectives O'Neill and Riker arrived from New Jersey, and along with them a swarm of reporters who had been covering their every move for almost two weeks.

The detectives' position was an ambiguous one. While they wanted Mrs. Martin as a material witness in New Jersey, they could not extradite her, having no proof that she had been in that state. In New York there was no charge against her.

It was somewhat timidly, therefore, that O'Neill knocked at the door of 855. "I wish to speak to you, Mrs. Martin," he said. "I am from a lawyer's office in East Orange."

"I cannot see you," said the answering voice. "How do you know that I am Mrs. Martin? I am not dressed to receive anyone."

The occupant steadfastly refused to open the door. Downstairs, reporters crowded the lobby. Fearing that they might impede further progress, police concocted a scheme to get rid of them. Manager Woodman told the press the woman in black had left through a back entrance. Meanwhile he was able to convince the occupant of 855 that she would be better off in a room on the seventh floor.

The reporters were not so easily deceived. Checking the back exit of the Bayard they saw a seven-foot fence which anyone leaving would have to scale. It was an unlikely feat for an elderly woman weighing close to two hundred pounds. Without a word to the management, the press contingent decided to act on its own, climbing unobserved up a fire escape to the eighth floor. To their surprise 855 was open and its occupant gone. One sharp-eyed newspaperman caught sight of an item left behind — a black tin box. As he and his colleagues devoured its contents, they knew they had stumbled on the most sensational evidence yet to come to light in the macabre case.

First came a large batch of clippings all related to the murder of Ocey Snead. Next came hotel receipts showing where Mrs. Martin, or Maybrick, or Lydig as she signed herself in one case, had spent recent weeks. On November 29, the day the dead body was reported to police, she had checked into the Martha Washington, at 23rd Street and Lexington Avenue and remained until December 9. From the ninth to the fourteenth she had been at the Hotel Aldine, at 431 Fourth Avenue, Manhattan. On the fourteenth she had checked into the Bayard.

Beneath these items of recent provenance lay the documents which caused the reporters to gasp — three suicide notes all written in the same hand! The first began almost like the one found in the East Orange house:

Last year my little daughter died. Other near and dear kindred, too, have gone to Heaven. I long to go there. I have been very weak and ill a long time. Death will be a blessed relief to me in my suffering. When you read this I will have committed suicide. My sorrow and pain in this world are greater than I can endure.

OCEY W. M. SNEAD

My little daughter has died, began the second note. *Other near and dear ones have died. I wish to join them in Heaven. I have been prostrated with illness a long time. When you read this I will be dead from suicide. Do not grieve for me. Rejoice with me that death brings me a painless sleep, a blessed relief from suffering and pain greater than I can bear.*

OCEY W. M. SNEAD

Addressed to *My Family,* the third despairing note read:

Because I feel my life ebbing away from sickness and suffering and losses, I feel the urgent necessity of hastening my own death by my own hand by a means I have hid from everyone. I would die away from the natural cause of sickness, but I cannot endure longer the suffering of this lingering death, and so I will myself end my own life at the very earliest opportunity that I can find. I alone am responsible for this because my suffering and losses and bereavement are so great. No living person is to blame for my death or has had anything to do with causing my death, which is due to my being unable to endure the suffering and losses and bereavement.

Ocey W. M. Snead

The small letter *r* and the capital *D* in the handwriting appeared to be almost identical to the script in the original suicide note. The shading of the letters was the same and the punctuation done with the same care. Even the color of the ink apparently matched. As in the bathtub note, the writing was in a steady, clear hand which betrayed not the slightest wavering or nervousness.

While reporters rushed to telephone their city desks, chagrined detectives arrived to take charge of the explosive new evidence. After examining it, they sent word to Prosecutor Wilbur Mott in East Orange. Mott immediately issued a warrant for the arrest of Mrs. Martin. During the day the various fencing procedures between press, police, the hotel management, and the woman in black had all consumed time. It was nine in the evening, Wednesday, December 15, when Detective O'Neill and Detective Skelly of the New York force pounded on the door of Mrs. Martin's seventh-floor room.

"I command you to open in the name of the law," Skelly said loudly. "I have a warrant for your arrest."

At first the occupant refused to comply. As the officers began to break down the door, it suddenly opened, revealing an upset and excited veiled figure.

"They cannot arrest me and take me to East Orange against my will. I will not go. I have some rights and they will be protected," Mrs. Martin said defiantly.

When Detective Skelly read the warrant of arrest, she appeared on the verge of collapse. The two officers supported her, one on each side, as they took her down the elevator, through the front entrance to a taxi, and off to the Mercer Street police station. Swaying as she left the cab, the aged heavy-set woman had to be held up.

Inside the station she walked down a long corridor to the detective bureau, where she was seated in a chair facing the desk of Lieutenant Funston. As she listened to him charge her with complicity in the slaying of Ocey Snead and with being a fugitive from justice, she trembled convulsively, lacing and relacing her fingers.

"I expected this but it is shameful," she said to the police officers around her. "I know you have to obey your orders but it is terrible that innocent and decent persons should be dragged through the streets and disgraced in this manner. I hope your mothers will never be placed in such a shameful position as the one that now faces me."

She at first objected to the lieutenant's questions and said she would discuss nothing until she had a lawyer to advise her. When told Franklin Fort would send an attorney to represent her next morning, she answered with her name, gave her age as 64 years, and her country of birth as the United States. Her occupation, she said, was "housekeeper." Asked to give her residence, she almost sobbed, "I have no home."

"Where is the great and wonderful McCafferty?" she suddenly demanded in a more challenging tone, referring to the chief police inspector. "I have read a great deal about him." An officer said the inspector was out of the building. "Oh, well, it doesn't matter," she sighed.

After being told that she would be arraigned in the morning in the Tombs police court, the weary prisoner was taken to her cell, where a matron asked if she had any needs. "Only a glass of water," came the reply. Mrs. Martin drank eagerly but held her veils with one hand so that her face, even at this midnight hour, might be protected. Then, fully clothed, she stretched out on a cot and slept.

A small irony in this latest unfolding of the case eluded police. At the Bayard, the woman in black had given, wittingly or unwittingly, a name famous in the annals of crime. Mrs. Florence Elizabeth Maybrick was the American wife of a Liverpool cotton broker who died at his home on May 11, 1889, under mysterious circumstances. Fiercely protesting her innocence, she was accused of poisoning her husband with arsenic, brought to trial, convicted, and sentenced to death. The sentence was commuted to penal servitude for life, then overruled by the British Home Secretary in 1904. Doubt as to his wife's guilt stemmed from the fact that Maybrick was known to use both strychnine and arsenic in small doses for their tonic and aphrodisiac effect. On her release, Mrs. Maybrick returned to her native state of Alabama, for like Mrs. Martin she was the daughter of an old and proud Southern family.

17

BY MORNING THE PRISONER was wonderfully refreshed, almost miraculously suffused with new energy. When the matron told her that reporters from two states were anxiously waiting, she said she would meet them forthwith. The press conference which ensued showed her at her beguiling best, speaking fluently and persuasively, answering questions with literary references, with cogent reasoning, with wit and charm, and all in all giving the performance of a consummate actress. It was clear that she had carefully followed the press coverage of the case; the New York *World* was evidently her favorite. The reporter from that paper opened the session, with succeeding queries coming from more than a score of men.

"Why have you been hiding, Mrs. Martin?"

"We are not yet so accustomed to our humiliations as to face them openly, but we are not crushed. There are animals whose first instinct when in pain is to run and hide their heads in some secluded spot. Others cry aloud so all can hear. It is the nature of my sisters and myself to be in silence, alone with God. I kept out of sight because I feared arrest. I have some property in Louisville on which I can get sixty-four hundred dollars to pay for attorney's fees. I wanted to convert this little property into cash for my sister's defense. I knew that if I were held even as a witness, I would have little opportunity to do the writing necessary to dispose of my property or obtain a loan on it."

"Did anyone know where you were? Franklin Fort or your sisters, for example?"

"Fort never knew. Neither did my sisters. They would never lie. I wrote Mary but never signed my name or told her my address."

"Why have you and your sisters behaved so mysteriously?"

"Why all this mystery? When I had money and lived here I visited and was visited by the Astors, Vanderbilts, and other leading families of the city. We could not bear for them to know that we were reduced to such poverty and facing such charges. None of us thought there would be more than some questions by the police, and so would say nothing. And there wouldn't have been but for the activity of the insurance companies."

"Why didn't you go to your daughter's funeral? There was no warrant out for your arrest in New York at the time."

"On the day that my daughter was buried I was in a little room in a boardinghouse, alone, and so ill from bodily sickness and mental anguish that I could not leave my bed. I had nothing but the horrible printed accounts of my predicament to keep me company. I am a woman sixty-four years old who until now has always held her head high. I also had little money and for three weeks until the time of my arrest I had hardly eaten a single bite."

"How did Ocey Snead die?"

"I am going to tell the facts about my daughter because it is time that the truth were known. My daughter Ocey came to her death by her own hand. I did not see her do it. I did not know that it was done until my sister was arrested, but I was not surprised. I had expected it for many months, ever since her husband, Fletcher, went away. During all those months of her life the desire to commit suicide became her ruling passion. She read every story of suicide in the news. When she could get books pertaining to suicide and crime, she absorbed every word of them. And she calmly told us that she intended to die soon. I have caught her writing out plans of suicide many times. She has written to all members of the family when we have been absent from New York, also to her cousins in the South, that when they read the letter she would be dead. I begged her over and over again not to write such things that would only cause much sorrow, but she held to her purpose. She told me many times that no matter how closely she was watched and guarded she would manage to elude us."

"But why write so many suicide notes, all similar?"

"It is the custom of educated and refined people to leave notes upon committing suicide. The illiterate and unrefined rarely do. It was perfectly natural then for her to make the note she left as nearly perfect as she could. It seems to me a most natural thing to do."

"If your daughter was going to commit suicide, why did she have a washrag in her hand?"

"The washcloth in my child's hand may be accounted for in at least two ways. She was one of the daintiest persons in the world. She would be spotlessly clean even in death, and perhaps took the bath before killing herself. Or it is quite possible that her aunt had thrown the cloth into the tub and it drifted into her half open hand. The police said her hand was not clutched to it."

"Some people — I have been told Prosecutor Mott among them — believe that you are the author of the suicide notes."

"Do you believe that if I or my sisters were guilty of crime we would keep such evidence, so easy to destroy? We may be old and foolish women, but we certainly are not so crazy as that would prove us to be. I can show you at least twenty-five suicide notes Ocey wrote. She used to keep them under her pillow."

"Why did your sister not go upstairs to see about your daughter when she knew she had suicidal tendencies?"

"Virginia knew less about the suicidal tendencies than I did. She did know that my daughter was extremely nervous. She had been asked to be left alone for twenty-four hours. Miss Wardlaw did not go upstairs because the steps were doubtless creaky and she feared to wake so light a sleeper. Miss Wardlaw is one of the most honorable of women. If told not to disturb one until a certain time, she would almost as soon have her hand cut off as to do it. She would hardly enter the room to give an alarm of fire if possible to give it in any other way."

"Why did your sister go to visit Dr. Teeter so late at night to get a health certificate?"

"As for Miss Wardlaw's going to see Dr. Teeter at ten o'clock for a health certificate, doubtless my daughter was uneasy about herself, and her friends here and elsewhere

were uneasy for her, and Miss Wardlaw wanted to assure
the patient and her friends that she was suffering from nothing but a little cold, as the doctor said. She would also be
cheered by the presence of the doctor."

"What about Fletcher Snead?"

"Fletcher left home last spring with Ocey expecting her
baby. She said write every day. Fletcher was supposed to testify against a Mr. Earthman of Nashville, with whom he had
been associated in business. What a splendid man he was!
He was so rich he couldn't count his money! The families
were so friendly that my sister Virginia had a drawing account in Earthman's bank at one time of ten thousand dollars. Fletcher said he'd rather die than make the trip. He
said if he didn't write every day we would know something
had happened to him. From that day, we heard no word.
We made inquiry, but without money we couldn't do much.
Our crime, it appears, has been that of being poor."

"You were not always poor. Can you tell us what happened?"

"My father was a Methodist minister. He traveled a great
deal and had an income of fourteen thousand dollars a year.
My daughter Ocey — you will note I call her my daughter,
for I have been asked if she were really my daughter — was
born in New York in Murray Hill. The house was number 37
East 39th Street. My husband made twenty thousand dollars
a year. Across the street from us lived banker Colgate. Next
door was Mrs. Winslow of soothing syrup fame and fortune.
Ocey was educated in the Convent of the Sacred Heart and
later in the school formerly conducted by Sylvanus Reed.
She was educated to become the head of a young ladies'
seminary in the South that my sister had conducted so successfully. We did not wish her to do hard work. We intended that she should live in the drawing room. Then came
the financial panic, and the men of our family went crashing

to the wall. Our dream of splendor was over. Our little girl's destiny was changed. At this point Fletcher proposed. As childhood playmates at their grandmother's he had asked her many times. Her first reply was, 'No, no! I don't want to marry anybody. I am going to be a teacher.' Finally he won her love and, after their first child was born, her complete adoration."

"What about Fletcher's first wife? Why did he leave her?"

"The reasons for the separation were that she was much older, and there was constant friction with her family. I do not wish to be harsh but our family always believed that she and her sister looked upon 'those Snead boys,' as they were called, as a pretty good thing for two old maids to marry, and they were simply 'roped in.' "

"What about Fletcher's insurance?"

"Much has been said of the 'mysterious' Senator McLaurin, the beneficiary of his policies. The man is Rufus H. McLaurin, former brother-in-law of Fletcher, who was chiefly instrumental in separating the couple. This man instigated a lawsuit against Fletcher and the wife sided with her family. The divorce followed shortly after. Then Fletcher sold all of his policies outright to his wife's brother, McLaurin, for nine hundred dollars, making him the beneficiary. So you see this insurance of Fletcher, which McLaurin pays for, would hardly be beneficial to us."

"Did Fletcher marry your daughter twice?"

"Yes, they were married in Louisville in 1906 by the Reverend Dr. Hoge. This marriage was kept quiet because they wanted no communication with the family of the first wife. The ceremony was repeated in New York because the laws covering marriages between first cousins are different in different states, and they didn't want any doubt covering the birth of their child."

"Why was Ocey Snead so emaciated when she died?"

"Many harsh things have been said about the way we starved Ocey when living in the house in Flatlands. We starve her? We all loved her more than we loved our lives. The poor child starved herself. That was one of the ways she intended to do away with herself, if no other fashion offered. The vast quantities of milk we bought were all for her. She had milk, chipped beef, crackers, and fresh eggs costing five cents each. She was told by the doctors to eat the eggs raw and had been used for a long time to eat them that way. Night after night we went out to buy some delicacy for her, pleaded to have her eat, only to have her put us away, shaking her beautiful head and crying out pitifully that she didn't want to live, but to please let her go to heaven, where she believed Fletcher was. We had many physicians, as is well known. They all say she had no chronic disorder. That is true. Her only trouble was heart sickness, and that at last brought on mental illness from which she could not recover."

"Why did she make out so many wills?"

"I will now speak of the various wills of Ocey that so much has been made of by the police. Her first will was made to cover some property in Kentucky in favor of her grandmother. This property was sold, thus nullifying the will. The second will was to cover some property in Virginia, which was also sold. The third will was made when it was feared she might die after the birth of her baby. She did not wish that the family of Fletcher's first wife might in any way benefit from her death. With Fletcher missing, a part of her estate would go to his son by this wife unless she provided otherwise. It was necessary to draw the fourth and following wills on account of the actions of the lawyer Carabba. I believe that the changes that he made in the will were never made at the dictation of Ocey. He never was alone in the room with her. I did take the five dollars from him, it is true, but only as a loan, and he got a receipt. We never heard of the man Schwartzmann. The man he brought with him to our home he called Black. In all of these wills Ocey's grandmother was made the beneficiary, together with the child. To each of the codicils there was a carefully drawn memorandum of instructions to my mother regarding the bringing up of the child, and incorporated as part of the will."

"What about the insurance on Ocey Snead's life?"

"And now again about that life insurance that seems to have made such apparent monsters of all of us. We didn't want Ocey's life insurance. We did all in our power to get the child to live and be our little girl. When our money dwindled and dwindled we tried our best to get a cash surrender value on all her policies, in order that they might not be any further drain upon us. My mother finally took the matter up and we received a letter from President Kingsley of the New York Life Insurance Company that the only thing to do to get rid of them was to let them lapse, as they had already been borrowed on to the limit. We took these policies out when we had plenty of money and when we were, all of us, an easy mark for insurance agents."

"Was there any ill feeling between your daughter and her aunt, Virginia Wardlaw?"

"Ocey was a very accomplished girl. She was splendidly educated, could do almost anything — paint, draw, and sew beautifully. All this talent she absorbed from her aunt, Miss Wardlaw, who was her inseparable companion."

"If you have to stand trial, what do you think will happen?"

"Our case will be so simple that there can be nothing but our acquittal. But we want to be tried by a jury of our peers. We mean a jury of women, not by our lords and masters. All of the men who have dealt against us are like grown-up children. They know not what they do, unless they are controlled by the evil genius that seems to have pursued us for years. Everything that we touched in the South seemed to be desired by someone else for financial exploitation and it withered and died. We should not indulge in comparisons but I'll simply refer to other women who have been vilified unjustly. Mary Queen of Scots and Madame Roland were made to suffer and were then canonized. Joan of Arc was killed and then became a saint. And so with us. They can crucify us now, while we live, but there will be a day of reckoning by and by. I would welcome death. I am old and infirm and would like to die. I would like to go to heaven, where the innocent are. I am absolutely innocent of any crime."

The performance had been dazzling. Having delivered herself of opinions on virtually every aspect of the case, Mrs. Martin's energies suddenly seemed drained. A magisterial wave of the hand brought the matron, Mrs. Donner, to her side. The interview was over. Back in her cell, the prisoner ate a light breakfast of coffee, rolls, and grapes, then rested while awaiting her arraignment.

18

IN THE SECOND ROOM Mrs. Martin had occupied at the Bayard Hotel, police found a second improvised suitcase, crammed, to no one's surprise, with documents. Carefully folded in one corner was the sheet of a Cleveland paper's Sunday supplement, the illustrated lead story entitled "The Curious Things They Are Doing with Hypnotism." Also a series of letters addressed to the wealthy Mrs. Russell Sage, to clubwoman-philanthropist Mrs. Clarence Burns, to lawyer Samuel Untermyer, to Professors Libby and Van Dyke of Princeton and to two relatives, Mrs. O. S. Pollock and Mrs. R. B. Spindle in Virginia. These letters pleaded for help in the defense of Virginia Wardlaw.

Of greater interest was a packet of correspondence which indicated that Fletcher Snead might be in Canada and alive. Detectives were sent out to check through all leads.

Likewise, several letters to Mary Snead at 466 West 22nd Street came in for special attention. With them was found a document which read: "I authorize Mrs. Robert Martin to make any contracts binding me in any manner she may see fit, and to sign my name to any and all of said contracts. Mrs. Martin being my attorney, in fact, to transact business for me or to sign my name with the same binding force that I could sign said contracts myself." Dated February 1, 1906, the affidavit was signed "Mary W. Snead."

Prosecutor Mott now felt certain that Mrs. Martin was the guiding power of the family, but he also saw increasing evidence of Mary Snead's involvement in the case. The fact that she had rented the East Orange house, that she was subservient to Mrs. Martin, who had evidently been in constant touch with her, made her appear to the prosecutor as an accomplice, willing or unwilling, to the machinations of the sister. Furthermore, similarities of dress among the three women were clearly such that witnesses were often unsure which black-clad sister they had seen.

At one thirty on Thursday afternoon, December 16, East Orange's Sergeant O'Neill and Detective Skelly of New York went to 466 West 22nd Street. They presented Mary Snead with a warrant accusing her of being a fugitive from the jurisdiction of New Jersey, where she was wanted on a charge of complicity in murder. The frail little woman, sixty-one years old, made no attempt to resist arrest, accompanying Skelly on foot to Tenth Avenue, where he hailed a cab to police headquarters.

An incongruous scene took place as they alighted. Press photographers began snapping photos just as a band of girls from a nearby public school came along. Raising their hands and shouting, the girls begged to be in the pictures. "Must I face them?" the dejected Mary Snead asked, referring to the cameramen. "They won't get much through the veils," said Skelly. Hurrying past the photographers and the screaming girls, the detective took his prisoner inside, where her fingerprints were taken and her official photo made in the humiliating process called "mugging."

O'Neill remained behind at 466. Here he found the usual evidence of the collector's mania so characteristic of the three sisters. Two leather handbags contained newspaper clippings of the Snead case, of unusual wills probated, and of surprise bequests of money made by "newly rich" people.

Most significantly, O'Neill found still another batch of suicide notes, again in what appeared to be the same hand as that which penned the one found in the East Orange bathroom. By now there was a suicide note for almost every occasion, for each time of the year, to different members of the family, an all-purpose series unique in police experience.

To My Absent Husband, Fletcher Snead, read the address on one envelope, dated June 25, 1909, while the letter inside said:

Dear Husband:

If you do not come home to me and your baby, soon to be born, I intend to end my own life. I cannot stand the long strain on my whole being. You have been gone over two months without a word from you and my heart is breaking.

If you are alive and find this, meet me in heaven. God bless you and good-bye.

> *Your loving and devoted wife,*
> OCEY W. M. SNEAD

Another note was addressed *To Whoever Finds This.* After expressing dread of pain, it concluded, *Nobody has harmed me and I have harmed nobody. I love everybody and everybody loves me, but I cannot endure physical agony.* Other notes provided variations on the same theme.

Preoccupation with death was reflected in a statement addressed to *My Counsel and Attorneys,* a document evidently designed to smooth the way for the payment of insurance in the event of decease.

> *Months ago I wrote an appeal to be released from my obligation to the insurance company,* it began, *asked it to restore to me the greater part of the money that I had paid to it, and to take back its contracts. President Kingsley wrote in reply a letter declining to do this, and so the contracts continue between me and the insurance company. My policies are endowment policies. They were taken out in good faith, with the expectation that I would live to use the endowment, but I have become unexpectedly and fatally ill from the effect of two childbirths and of the death of my first child, and the severe illness of my second child. Promptly collect my insurance in cash and pay it over to my grandmother without requiring any bond or security from her.*
> OCEY W. M. SNEAD

A letter to Mrs. Clarence Burns, sponsor of the Federation Hotel for Working Girls where Ocey Snead had resided briefly in early 1909, showed a similar anticipation of death.

Dear Mrs. Burns —

On the few occasions that I had the pleasure of meeting you at the Federation Hotel you entirely won my heart. Your kindness of speech and cordial manner caused you to be loved by everyone. Your life is so full of noble, generous deeds that, like a fragrant flower, it sheds around a sweet aroma that gives pleasure to all within the favored circle. Since leaving the house I have been in Long Island. My husband has been very ill for a long time. I too, have not been well. You probably may remember that my stay at the house was only temporary. A little soul lies near my heart which I am expecting soon to be ushered into this strenuous world. I have a presentiment that I will not live through the ordeal.

If I should die as some mothers do, I bespeak your kindness for the motherless little one I may leave behind. You seemed to feel an interest in me which I deeply appreciate and I hope and believe you will be kind and sweet to my babe should it be left motherless. I am sorry I could not have known you better, but what I know of you led me to believe you would befriend one who needed a friend.

Sincerely,

OCEY W. M. SNEAD

As indicated, while Franklin Fort saw the many letters and notes dealing with suicide and death as signs that Ocey Snead had long contemplated doing away with herself and therefore as proof of the three sisters' innocence, Wilbur Mott viewed them from a diametrically opposed angle.

"Let me tell you that the murder of Ocey Snead was to have been committed in the Flatlands of Brooklyn," the prosecutor explained as he prepared to arraign his two new prisoners. "In my opinion the family went out there for no other purpose. Dr. Pettit stood between this girl and her death in Brooklyn at that time. When Dr. Pettit and the nurse he brought to the house became suspicious, the women became afraid and gave up the job for the time being. There is no doubt in my mind that this crime in East Orange was a long time hatching. That is the explanation of those suicide letters. They were a part of the conspiracy and were designed to disarm the police."

Mott showed reporters a note signed "Ocey W. M. Snead." One of the items found in the Bayard Hotel, it read:

To My Executor —
In consideration of the kindness to me of Dr. William R. Pettit, and his treatment of me during my illness, I direct you to pay him $1,000 upon my death.

It was inconceivable, according to Mott, that Ocey Snead actually had written this note, giving Dr. Pettit ten times his fee, since she had received no special attention and was probably too weak even to lift her hand. The offer of a thousand dollars had been made by the sisters with the intent of getting at least passive aid from the doctor toward evil ends.

"I regard the application at ten o'clock at night to Dr. Teeter for a health certificate for Ocey Snead also as a strong point against the sisters," Mott continued. "Miss Wardlaw's lawyer tells me she sought it to send to her mother, Ocey's grandmother, so the latter would know Ocey was getting along all right. I told him such an explanation was absurd. If there were no suspicions against Miss Wardlaw, the strongest possible assurance to the grandmother that Ocey was well would be a line from the aunt. Common sense will tell you there was another reason for obtaining that certificate late in the night, when the doctor protested against going, and when this woman, though apparently without the barest necessities of life, paid cab hire and a doctor's fee.

"Bearing out Dr. Pettit's statements that Ocey Snead was neglected when ill, the tin box in my safe, taken from the Bayard Hotel, contains prescription after prescription unfulfilled. I have also in my possession nearly one hundred wills purported to have been made by the girl, some executed and some not. All these things convince me that the plot had its beginning many months ago. Who can conceive of a person having written a suicide note, and all nerved up to the point of taking her life, getting into the bathtub with a washcloth in her hand? That tragedy was too well planned."

He had been gathering evidence to prove that both Mrs. Martin and Mary Snead had been in East Orange in the period before the dead body was found, said Mott. Some of his material would be presented at the arraignment of the two prisoners scheduled for that afternoon, December 16. The prosecutor expressed confidence it was strong enough to warrant extraditing them from New York into his jurisdiction.

19

AS PREPARATION FOR THE HEARING GOT UNDER WAY, the two sisters in black came into the courtroom — Mary Snead shy and reserved, Caroline Martin making a dramatic entrance, black banners flying. She had had several hours for reflection. The upshot was a thoroughly sour disposition.

"The police of this city represent in blue coats and brass buttons the barbarism of the Spanish Inquisition set into modern times," she began coldly as she recalled her experiences of the previous night. "Where is my lawyer? Where is the black box I left in the Hotel Bayard? Someone has been tampering with it. I know someone has been tampering with it, and they must give back what was taken out.

"Why the delay?" she demanded when proceedings did not begin immediately. A bailiff explained they were waiting for A. Gilbert, the lawyer Franklin Fort had asked to represent them.

"Is he good? I don't know him," came another querulous response.

"He is supposed to be excellent," said the bailiff.

"I don't know yet if Mr. Fort has thrown me over," Mrs. Martin continued, directing her remark to a nearby Newark *Evening Star* reporter. "If he has deserted me, I will select another lawyer. Can you give me a list of good criminal lawyers? I positively will not be bothered with cheap lawyers."

Before an answer could be given, Magistrate Cornell made his entrance into the room and opened the court. He was soon to find Mrs. Martin a skillful legal fighter, dogged in protecting her legal rights and astute at winning the sympathy of many around her. The magistrate explained that the hearing was a formality, legally required so that he could keep them in custody and remand them back into the Tombs Prison while awaiting extradition to New Jersey. At the railing the energetic Mrs. Martin was on her feet as soon as he had finished, moving with a swiftness that belied her heavy frame.

"Judge, we are two poor women without friends and without counsel," she pleaded. "We appeal to you to protect our rights."

"Why haven't you counsel?"

"We are too poor."

"If that is true, I will do anything I can for you."

"What is the charge against me?" asked Mrs. Martin, continuing the offensive.

"There are two warrants against you. They were read to you last night at your arrest. You are wanted as fugitives from justice by the state of New Jersey."

"But my sister was not in New Jersey when this alleged crime was committed. There are dozens of witnesses to prove it. Nor was I. We are citizens of this state. Have we, as persons accused, no rights?"

"Yes."

"Must you hold me because the New Jersey authorities ask you to do so?"

"For a reasonable time."

"As a matter of courtesy?"

"No, as a matter of law."

"We have nothing to do with each other," said Mrs. Martin in a surprise shift, pointing to her sister. "I haven't seen this woman for a long time, not until she came to the Tombs. I know little of her. Our cases are entirely separate."

"Madam, the question of facts is not our concern at this moment. I am informed that the Essex County grand jury will consider your case next Tuesday. Now I cannot hold you by law for more than forty-eight hours at a time. The only question before us is whether you are willing to stay in the Tombs until Wednesday, when the jury's action will be known, or whether I must bring you before me again in forty-eight hours."

"Is your information oral or official?"

"The question is: Are you willing to stay in the Tombs or must I bring you before me again in forty-eight hours?"

"What power have I in the matter? Is it any advantage to me to consent to leave it until Wednesday? I have no lawyer. I don't know my rights."

"You can do whatever you wish."

"Well, wouldn't it be a tacit consent on my part to await grand jury proceedings?"

"Yes."

"Owing to the absence of my counsel, I will return in forty-eight hours. I will return as often as necessary rather than sacrifice any of my rights. Will you let me see the warrant from New Jersey?"

"I will read it to you," said the magistrate and proceeded to do so, ending his account with the name of the East Orange recorder, Francis Nott.

"Is it not Francis Nott, *Jr.?*" asked the alert woman in black.

"It is," Cornell was forced to admit, to her obvious satisfaction.

"I would like to look at it myself," Mrs. Martin said. "I am so nervous and my sight is so bad that I would like to have the book in my cell in prison so I can read it thoroughly."

"Step down and your further questions will be answered presently."

"Just a minute, you men," Mrs. Martin shouted at the bailiffs who were taking her by the arms. "I am in the hands of the judge now. He is speaking to me."

"Step down off the bridge, madam."

Reluctantly the prisoner left the bridge and took her seat. In a moment she was up again and calling across the room to the magistrate, but to no avail.

Sergeant William O'Neill led Charles Kirk to the witness stand. The young boy, of Eaton Place and Fourteenth Street in East Orange, had spoken of a woman in black whom he had seen near his home, identifying her as Virginia Wardlaw. This had evidently been a case where the two sisters were confused by a witness. Kirk later recalled a slight limp in the woman's walk, a characteristic which would identify her as Mrs. Martin.

"Is that the woman who on November 29 offered you first five and then ten cents to carry a bundle from the North

Fourteenth Street house?" asked Magistrate Cornell, pointing at Mrs. Martin. While an attendant lifted the startled prisoner's veil, the boy gazed on a powerful alert face, the sharp eyes peering through foggy spectacles, challenging his, only the finely wrinkled skin, brown as ancient parchment, betraying advanced years.

"It is," answered the boy.

"It is a manufactured lie," the prisoner corrected him.

It was the only question addressed to the boy. Already on file, said the magistrate, was an affidavit swearing that Mary Snead had rented the East Fourteenth Street house. These two facts were sufficient to warrant holding the sisters pending extradition.

"By what provision of the code am I held, your honor?" demanded Mrs. Martin, rising once again to her feet.

"I will show you the court order," the judge patiently answered and sent it along by an attendant.

"I want to see the text of the code, please, since I must be my own lawyer," said Mrs. Martin.

"Give her this," said the judge, handing over the code book opened at the proper place. "And take the woman out."

"Let me go, let me go," cried the bulky Mrs. Martin, resisting attendants' efforts to remove her. "I have a right to speak to the judge. I am a retired schoolteacher of this city. I deserve better treatment."

"Come along now. Don't make a fuss," said one of the attendants.

"Judge, I demand fair treatment," shouted the prisoner.

The struggle that ensued was a tragicomic entertainment for the court. Writhing, sliding her feet heavily on the floor, Mrs. Martin tried to hold her ground. Detectives took her arms. Still she managed to seize the benches on either side of her, to hook a foot into the cast-iron underpinning, to cling there a moment, immovable, a squat figure in her loose black Mother Hubbard gown. Miss Coleman, one of the prison matrons, made an attempt at oral persuasion, but in vain. Two detectives tried to lift and carry the prisoner. At this point she simply let her entire weight drop to the floor. Six burly men in blue now joined forces, lifting her bodily and carrying her out of the room. She had not screamed, or struck anyone, or even lost her temper, but her opposition had been formidable.

From the courtroom a narrow overhead passageway called the Bridge of Sighs led across the street into the Tombs Prison. The policemen carried Mrs. Martin the entire distance. Mary Snead walked along behind, silently. She was taken to the cell next to that of her sister. When the door closed behind her, she began softly to cry.

20

ONE OF THE MISSING LINKS IN THE CASE, Fletcher Snead, had become the object of endless rumor and speculation as the days went by. It was clear that he and his wife Ocey had come to New York a year and a half ago, staying first in good hotels such as the Brevoort and in well-located private houses. Later, the living arrangements had declined, along with those of the rest of the family.

Fletcher had been employed by the Corbin Construction Company as an office clerk. A likable man, he was not particularly adept at his work. His wife Ocey was known to come to his office on Sundays to help him bring his accounts up to date. "He seemed to have something on his mind," said the company's owner, John R. Corbin, who finally discharged him early in 1909.

Not long after, a federal marshal sought to subpoena him as a witness in the case of *W. B. Earthman & Company vs. the First National Bank of Murfreesboro*. Fletcher had worked for Earthman, who was charged with looting the bank of which he was president, of using his position to get funds for his personal use. Through a lawyer, Fletcher asked to be excused from appearing, pleading illness. Within the month, March 1909, he left New York.

While his wife and relatives expressed the view that he had died, contrary reports kept cropping up. In Memphis, Tennessee, William Brantley Smith, a portrait painter who knew the family, said he had seen Fletcher only a month ago on a trip to Europe. In New York, merchants in several neighborhoods where Fletcher had lived said they had seen him recently in the street, looking haggard and ill. Other accounts placed him in hospitals and one said he had been committed to prison.

So much of the case had been fought in the newspapers that it came as no great surprise when it was reporters who found Fletcher Snead, alive, in a small Canadian town across the border from Niagara. At St. Catherine's, Ontario, the scion of the distinguished Wardlaw and Snead families was discovered working as a second cook, his aristocratic profile blurred by a reddish beard, his five-foot-ten frame slim and almost scrawny. To his fellow employees at the New Murray Hotel, he was known as John Lucas.

Proprietor Samuel Barnett recalled his arrival in late April of the year. His wife was dead, he had said, and also his baby. To Barnett he appeared a defeated man, but clearly of a good background. When he asked him why he did not pull himself up, Lucas had replied, "Oh, I've seen the upper strata and I am content with what I now have."

The only job open at the time was that of second cook.

Lucas said he didn't care what kind of work it was, so long as it was work. He eagerly took the opening in the kitchen and the owner had no fault to find with his performance of his duties. Although he was not very communicative, everyone liked him. They wondered a bit about the three personal towels he had brought along marked *Snead.* Each time they passed through the laundry, they caused comment.

The girls working in the kitchen naturally took an interest in the nice-looking young man. They found no reciprocity on his part. When one of them asked if he had a "steady," she was surprised by the vehemence of his reply. "No, good God, no," he said. "No women for me. They have ruined my life. I never want to see another woman."

In June, however, he had a female visitor. Heavily veiled, wearing black, she had inquired about John Lucas before registering as "Mrs. Ball, Cleveland." After viewing one room she returned to the desk dissatisfied and asked for cheaper accommodations. A second-floor assignment was more to her liking. Although it was against the rules, she insisted that Lucas come to see her in the room. The young man, upset on hearing of her presence, nevertheless hurried to obey her. For three days, whenever he was off duty, he spent his time with the elderly woman. When she left, he walked with her to a streetcar and was heard to say, "Remember, this is the last time." The young cook appeared troubled in spirit for many weeks thereafter. To his boss he announced he might soon have to be away for a few days as he expected his grandmother would leave him some money.

Reports of the mysterious John Lucas spread through the town and filtered across the border. By Thursday, December 16, reporters from New York and New Jersey newspapers began to descend on St. Catherine's. When they confronted John Lucas, he turned pale and at first refused to deny or affirm his identity. One reporter showed him the front page of a paper with a photo of Mrs. Martin.

"It is she. It is Aunty who visited me here," he said. His hands trembled as he held the page; tears filled his eyes. "It was most kind of you to show me the paper. I cannot make a statement. I will not. I dare not. I left it all behind and I am not going back to it. The past is dead to me. I am not Fletcher Snead in the real sense of the word. Fletcher Snead is dead to all appearances. I am John Lucas and will be regarded as such. When I came here and changed my name that ended me as Fletcher W. Snead."

Reporters were unable to draw further information from the bearded young man, who shuddered as he retreated to his room. Although he continued to do his work, he now spoke hardly at all, even to the employees of the hotel. However, a day after his discovery a telegram was delivered to him from his mother.

"By some unaccountable mistake there have appeared unquestionable falsehoods concerning us that will do all of us the greatest possible injury," it read. "I adjure you to take heart and have no fear for all will yet be well. We do not ask you to come to us. You know the best what to do."

In a shabby servant's room of the hotel, newspapermen found him with the cable. In the storm of sobs he whispered over and over again, "My poor little wife Ocey and my dear mother." To the journalists he said, "Tell my mother I'll come back to her, that I have not deserted her. Tell that to my aunts, too — also that I have saved my money for them to use in their hour of need."

Breaking his silence, he clarified his position. He had left his wife in March of the year, worked in a cheap New York restaurant for several months to accumulate money, then had gone directly to St. Catherine's. En route he changed his name to John Lucas, the name of his great-grandfather. His purpose in leaving was not to desert his wife and family, whom he loved, but simply to avoid testifying in the federal case against William Earthman.

"It may seem ridiculous that I would go to such lengths," he volunteered. "People of the North cannot understand. William Earthman was the best friend I had on earth. In my childhood I had been dandled on his knee. I loved him like a father. He called me his son. When I started in business in the South he helped me in every way, and I made what was considered a fortune in the lumber business. Then they subpoenaed me to testify against him for breaking United States banking laws. I told my wife, my mother, my aunts, I would die before doing that, that the whole United States could not make me do it. My life has since been a perfect hell with worry over my family, but I tell you, and oh, I hope you will believe me, it was my idea of the honorable thing to do. It was inborn. I could not help it.

"Southern pride was at the heart of the matter," Fletcher Snead insisted. It accounted for the family's saying to everyone that he was dead, although they had no confirmation of such a fact. It was to protect Earthman that they said so. "Even to my wife I became dead," he explained. "They have not lied in saying that I was dead, even though it has been shown that my aunt visited me here in June. Fletcher Snead was dead and for them to never admit otherwise was their idea of honor. There has been no mystery in our family. We have just been proud and clannish enough to attend to our own affairs, and nobody ever thought of it till now."

Mystery certainly did seem a family specialty, despite his disavowal. He had been married to his wife, he said, not once, not twice, but actually three times. The first ceremony was secret and after it he and Ocey did not live together for more than a year. The second ceremony, in Louisville, was also kept quiet because his first wife threatened trouble. And the third marriage, in New Jersey, took place because as first cousins he and Ocey wanted to make sure of their status before the birth of their child.

Trouble with his first wife, said Fletcher, was the result of "the old story of the wife's family. My quarrel with her brother, McLaurin, to whom I then sold my life insurance policy, went so far that I once had the pleasure of looking down the barrel of a revolver held in his hand. But my love for Ocey made up for all of that."

The mention of the name Ocey brought a look at once tender and despairing to Fletcher Snead's eyes. "Dear little girl, I always called her my sweet child," he exclaimed. "I loved her with all my heart. Can't you understand and believe that? I don't know why she wanted to die by her own hand, but I am willing to take oath that so far as I know that is how she did die. Not a member of the family ever forged those letters. My Aunt Caroline writes an irregular scrawling hand and could never imitate the neat penmanship of Ocey. I wasn't kept informed how things were going. I admit that. My Aunt Caroline is peculiar. I admit that. I have had some experience with her to know, but she had a heart that is as big as the world and she loved her child almost as much as I did. I don't believe for a minute that she or my Aunt Virginia murdered my wife. She thought the world of them and they did of her. They are as fine women as can be found anywhere. All this talk of hypnotism is utter and absolute rot. Neither my mother nor my aunts knew the art.

"We are all poor. That is where we made our mistake — to ever lose our money. The day before the panic of 1907 I went to bed worth thousands of dollars. The next day I was penniless. Earthman went down in the same crash. I came to

New York to build over again and the result — ah, you would think I had had enough of life to join Ocey, wouldn't you?

"I think of my little child every hour," he went on. "I have never seen it and yet I love it with all the love that a father should have. I will go to it some day and claim it."

On this plaintive note the interview ended, with Fletcher Snead stretched out on his cot, his body racked with sobs.

The evocation of painful memories had taken its toll. He was unable to report for work. The next day, when a friend, businessman C. Watts, arrived from New York to persuade him to return with him, he flatly refused. Authorities in Canada said they would keep him under surveillance but had no grounds for further action. In New Jersey Wilbur Mott said he did not believe him to be involved in the alleged murder conspiracy and therefore had no plans to bring him across the border. In the afternoon, Fletcher Snead — or rather, John Lucas — reported as usual for his shift as cook in the New Murray Hotel.

21

"His affairs are his own," said Mrs. Martin when told that her nephew was remaining in Canada. "He has nothing to do with our troubles. We hold no bitterness toward him. We love him. My daughter still loves him in her home in heaven. I do not say that he should come here, much as I have longed to see him. I would not interfere with him in any way."

The older sister, restless in her prison cell, spent a good deal of time talking to Mary Snead. Guards detected a certain coldness developing, however, after the latter learned her sister had actually gone to visit Fletcher at a time when she and Ocey and others of the family thought him dead. Mrs. Martin must have found an effective way of explaining her actions. Soon she and Mary Snead were again chatting in a genial manner.

The two sisters read a great deal as the legal wheels turned around them, Mrs. Martin especially devouring all the newspaper accounts of the Snead case, retaining the clippings. In the interviews she granted to her favorite reporters, a robust sense of persecution paranoia manifested itself, her main oppressors being the police, the lawyers, and the insurance companies.

"The police have robbed me of my papers," she announced on Friday, December 17. "They have built up a case which I cannot fight against. When they found that I was not represented by counsel they brought a boy to say that I had been in New Jersey. There is no evidence to show that I was implicated in my daughter's death, and if I had the money these men would never dare to hold me on a charge of murder. I can prove that every bit of evidence brought against my two sisters has been presented by the big interests who want to cheat us out of our money."

The almighty dollar in her view was at the root not only of all evil but of everything, and in a summing up she reached poetic heights of expression: "The only use the world has for a widow who is old — old — is to see how much money she has and to then get it. Money. Think of the terrible potency of it. You can't do anything without money. You can't be born without money. You can't be married without money. You can't move your hand to your face without money. You can't even die without money. I considered that money alone would gain my sister's liberty and I tried to get it before my arrest.

"Ocey Snead was insured for some twenty thousand dollars," she said, "and the millionaire insurance men are willing to spend ten thousand dollars in hiring detectives and lawyers so as to save for their pockets the other. If we had been rich, the money would have been paid without question. Prosecutor Mott is a fine man, they tell me, but he is being deceived and hoodwinked by those highly paid detectives of the insurance companies. Those men who own the insurance companies, millionaires and multimillionaires, are anxious to prevent three old women from coming into the money that they deserve. Prosecutor Mott sits on one side of the table and the insurance company detectives on the other, and they pass under the table to him these alleged scandalous findings that they have unearthed about the family. Then they are passed out to the newspapers by the prosecutor, and my sisters and I are held up to public ridicule as three Siamese twins. It's like the vivisectionists. They cut up and kill poor, helpless animals just to ascertain how they can help human beings to live. The insurance companies are practicing vivisection on me and my sisters, deceiving themselves into believing that in order that they may live three old women must die. If the prosecutor will only visit me at the Tombs I will tell him all.

"Without ever having seen my lawyer or knowing what sort of man he was, and helpless, I wrote him a telegram of several hundred words, telling my predicament and urging him to come to me at once. They wouldn't send it.

"The letters written by Ocey were proof that she committed suicide, and no matter how many witnesses are called to drag us before a judge, we can show our persecutors have not even allowed us private communication with counsel. Every word is overheard by spies who give distorted statements to the police."

The elderly woman's ramblings had a solid basis in fact.

The insurance companies did, in fact, still refuse to pay the money on Ocey Snead's policies. The prosecution did, in fact, release long statements to the press. At the Thursday hearing, the sisters were, in fact, unrepresented by counsel. As it happened, Fort, otherwise occupied, had asked A. S. Gilbert of the law firm of Mayer and Gilbert to counsel the sisters. Gilbert had made a mistake in timing and arrived after the hearing was over.

"The authority of the police here appears to be greater than in Russia," declared Fort, who appeared as indignant as his client. "The question of attorney privileges raised by the taking of papers in this case I consider more important than the question of acquittal or conviction of the defendants. If suppression of mail, opening of letters, and interruption of communication between counsel and client have been permitted in this case, there will be important developments."

After an interval of forty-eight hours, as required by New York law, the two sisters were brought back into court. This time, on Saturday, December 18, Franklin Fort was at their side. In appearance they were much as before save for a curious circumstance. From a prison matron it was learned the two sisters had exchanged veils. Since their veils were so much alike, courtroom spectators were not aware of the subtle shift of accessories.

New Jersey authorities presented a new series of witnesses to testify that Mary Snead and Caroline Martin were in East Orange about the time of the death of Ocey Snead. The sisters were asked to stand in a line with other women prisoners as these witnesses came into the courtroom, a procedure which infuriated Mrs. Martin.

"They will not see my face," she shouted as a matron forcibly drew up first her veils, then those of Mary Snead. "I have some rights and the police cannot force me to stand here for inspection. Get out of here! You're trespassers."

The witnesses nonetheless came forth. Druggist John B. Foster of 401 Seventh Avenue, East Orange, identified Mary Snead as the woman who applied at his store shortly before the tragedy for a list of nearby physicians. Mary Quimby, a clerk in his employ, confirmed his statement. Real estate agent A. H. B. Harper testified that Mary Snead had tried to rent one of his houses in Arlington, New Jersey, before taking the North Fourteenth Street house in East Orange. He recalled that in both instances she had commented on the size of the bathtub.

"Of course they will recognize me. I am dressed in black," Mrs. Martin complained as two additional witnesses came to inspect her. "Can't I change my clothes? This is not fair."

George Handschuh, conductor on the Roseville trolley line to Newark, identified Mrs. Martin as the woman who rode his car on the afternoon of November 29, the same day the body of Ocey Snead was found. She entered the car at Orange and Fourteenth, said Handschuh, and got off at High Street in Newark. He also recalled that she carried a rope-bound black bag.

Edward Henry, a young boy, recognized Mrs. Martin as a woman he saw near North Fourteenth Street at about four o'clock on November 29. Her curious appearance had intrigued him. As he watched her walk off, he said, he noted a piece of her black veil fluttering to the ground. After she was out of view, he picked it up. He had later brought it to the police.

"I don't see how the wind could have blown it off," Mrs. Martin interrupted. "It wasn't windy that day."

"How do you recall that it wasn't windy that particular day when you say you were not even in East Orange?"

The question gave Mrs. Martin pause for thought. Not to be led on in this dangerous area, she retreated into silence.

After the appearance of these witnesses, Magistrate Cornell once again remanded the two sisters to the Tombs. Earlier, Franklin Fort had said he would fight the extradition of Mary Snead but would not oppose that of Caroline Martin; now he said he would not oppose either move.

Later it was learned he had spoken to Virginia Wardlaw and was now sure that Mrs. Martin had indeed been in the East Orange house on November 29 and had left there shortly before four o'clock. From that moment until her discovery in the Bayard Hotel she had wandered about in New York and the surrounding area, keeping in touch with her sisters but not informing them of her precise whereabouts.

It was also learned that Mary Snead had said that all three sisters spent Sunday night, November 28, the day before Ocey's body was found, in the room at 466 West 22nd Street. There they had composed a letter to the Georgia Methodist Conference, asking to borrow money on a church pension which came to them through their father. Virginia Wardlaw, according to this account, had spent the night in New York and returned to East Orange on Monday. While this would account for Virginia's not having seen Ocey's dead body over a twenty-four-hour period, other occupants of the house were ready to swear that only Mary Snead and her aged mother were in the house on that crucial Sunday night.

Evidently Virginia Wardlaw had known of Mrs. Martin's Monday visit to the East Orange house, but had kept that fact hidden to protect her. Only because Mary Snead was now also in custody, and to try to prove her innocence, had she finally made the admission.

As Prosecutor Mott saw it, each new bit of evidence, each new frame of the changing picture pointed convincingly to the guilt of the sisters, all three. After a two-hour conference with Franklin Fort, who asked him to drop all charges, Mott made a statement.

"The state may ask why, with their knowledge of the suicide mania it is said the girl possessed, did her mother and her mother's sisters allow her to live alone in the East Orange house," he began. "The state will want to know why Ocey Snead was led to believe she never would hear from her husband, when one or more of these three old women knew where he was. It may ask why Mrs. Martin paid Fletcher a visit at a time when Ocey was grieving herself to death in the belief that her husband was dead. Assisting suicide is as much of a criminal offense as murder. It is the same act in fact. Suicide in English, you know, means self-murder, and aiding or abetting one to murder himself is murder in the eyes of the law."

The single suicide note found in the East Orange bathroom was no longer of such crucial importance since so many others had been found, said Mott. The factor now in the fore was the strange mental influence exerted on Ocey Snead when she wrote them. "I know positively that Mrs. Martin and the two sisters worked upon the girl's mentality until she became a wreck," he stated. "Letters she wrote that are in my possession prove she was deceived into believing her husband would not return. And every other influence calculated to reduce her to a melancholy and morbid state, producing suicidal mania, was brought to bear. In short, these women imbued the girl with the idea that the shadow of death was upon her. Then she was taken to a lonely, unfurnished house and afforded every opportunity to do away with herself.

"If I actually knew from an eyewitness that Ocey Snead pinned the suicide note on her clothing, got into the bathtub, and drowned herself, I would still go before the grand jury and demand indictments for murder against Mrs. Caroline B. Martin and her sisters Mrs. Snead and Miss Wardlaw. I know absolutely that even if the girl did commit sui-

cide, she did so at the instigation of these women, who
having aided and abetted, are guilty of murder."

In terms of specifics of the case, the prosecutor said: "We
expect to prove that for twenty-four hours after the death of
Ocey Snead, the mother and Miss Wardlaw were in that
house. Then, at four o'clock, the mother left. She went up to
Eaton Place and Fourteenth Street. She was on the way to
get a trolley car for Newark when she met the Kirk boy. She
accosted the boy. She lifted her veils. One of the several she
wore fell off. It was picked up by a person who lives in
Eaton Place and we regard it as a most valuable exhibit.

"Apparently the two women deliberated long on what to
do after the girl was dead. Then at four o'clock, having apparently reached a satisfactory conclusion, Mrs. Martin left
the house. We have her traced by the minute by a chain of
indisputable circumstances. She was seen by the Kirk boy
about four fifteen, which makes the approximate time of
leaving the house at four o'clock. We hope to be able to
trace her movements as she walked to take the trolley car to
Newark, where she got a train for New York, and went to
live at a hotel under an assumed name.

"When Mrs. Martin left the house, Miss Wardlaw was
alone with the body of Ocey Snead. There she waited for
some minutes, forty to be exact, until twenty minutes to five
o'clock before she notified the police. So you see how this fits
in. I am of the opinion that Miss Wardlaw delayed sending
the news to the police in order to give Mrs. Martin a chance
to get away, and that is what I am going to prove. There will
be no 'hypnotic suggestion' or any other kind of 'suggestion'
in the case as I will present it. I am firmly convinced that it
was a genuine, cold-blooded murder, and that is what I will
prove."

That omnivorous newspaper reader Mrs. Caroline Martin
read this interview with the prosecutor and immediately

contacted her lawyer. Assailing what she called the "subsidized press" and "New Jersey justice," she declared, "They
are trying to railroad me out of New York and into a New
Jersey prison on the most flimsy evidence." It was her inten-
tion, she said, to call in reporters and refute Mott. At this
point, Franklin Fort said it would not be in her own best
interests to talk to the press. Henceforth, he cautioned her,
she should speak about the case only to him.

The muzzle on her activities did not sit well with Mrs.
Martin, who had a definite knack and relish for the limelight. Hardly had Fort left when she told a New York *Daily
Tribune* reporter of her dilemma, expressing great regret at
Fort's injunction. The newspapers, after all, represented
thousands of people, and she felt sure they would help her if
they fully understood her case. Furthermore, she sympa-
thized with these masses, who wished to spend a penny or
two pennies to get the inside of a fascinating story.

"I want to talk but I am like one of the six hundred who
rode to their death through obeying orders," she said, allud-
ing to Tennyson's poem "The Charge of the Light Brigade."
"I do not mean that we are surely going to our death. We
are innocent. Money alone would secure our liberty. Every
way I turn they want money. The newspapers should act as
judges and not as prosecutors of three old women. I am writing a history of this case which may be given out at some
future time but for the present will be used to guide our
defense."

Her last admonition to the journalists was that their artists
should be more careful in reproducing her likeness. Their
drawings, she said, did not do her justice. In her cell Mrs.
Martin reflected further on Fort's decision not to fight extradition and on his order barring her from speaking to the
press. As a result of these musings she decided to fire him as
her counsel. In his place she secured the services of Robert

Haire, a veteran of many legal battles in the Western states who had numbered among his clients, at different times, both Frank and Jesse James. She would not take any chances on the New Jersey law, the prisoner told this new counsel, and asked him to fight to keep her in New York.

22

A RUDE SHOCK AWAITED THE ELDEST of the three sisters on Monday, December 20. "Mrs. Martin is insane," declared her discharged lawyer. Franklin Fort made the statement after another meeting with Virginia Wardlaw. "If Mary Snead had not been arrested, Miss Wardlaw would have gone to the chair rather than reveal her sister's insanity," he elaborated. "Now she feels it her sacred duty to tell all to clear Mrs. Mary Snead."

For twenty-five years Mrs. Martin had been mentally irresponsible, said Fort. At intervals the family wanted her committed to an insane asylum. Virginia Wardlaw opposed these plans, preferring to keep her at large although her financial manipulations again and again defeated various plans started by Virginia to rehabilitate the family finances. The eldest sister's mental disorder was at the bottom of the mystery of the bathtub tragedy and was the skeleton in the closet which the family had tried to hide for a quarter of a century. It accounted for the strange comings and goings of the Wardlaws, for the peculiar documents strewn over the landscape.

It was Virginia Wardlaw, said Fort, who played the martyr's role over these tragic and terrifying years. Twice she established successful school administrations in the South, only to have her sister dismantle them. As the eldest, Caroline had viewed it as her inherent right to supervise the finances of the schools. Virginia had tried to carry on even under her baleful influence but had been defeated. Over the years it was she who had tried to keep little Ocey beyond her mother's influence, but here too she had finally failed.

If the grand jury brought joint indictments against the three sisters, Fort said, he would ask them to be severed so that Mrs. Martin would have a separate trial.

"This case is so important that it seems to me if the question of the sanity of Mrs. Martin is raised, the question will have to be answered after the indictments," commented Wilbur Mott. "If Mrs. Martin held her relatives under a hypnotic spell it is up to the jury to decide."

The object of this interchange waxed indignant on hearing of it. On only one occasion, said Mrs. Martin, did members of her family speak of having her committed. She and her sisters had furnished funds for the education of John Snead. When he graduated, she said, he refused to reimburse her and she threatened to sue. If she did, he would charge her with insanity, the young man retorted. "The threat was childish," said Mrs. Martin.

"I am going to conduct my own case whether Mr. Fort likes it or not," she asserted with a confident air. "I have instructed Mr. Haire to institute habeas corpus proceedings in my case. Mr. Fort says I am insane. I am wise enough to keep away from New Jersey."

After a conference with his new client, Robert Haire had an announcement quite as startling as that made by Fort. "Ocey Snead was a dope fiend!" he said. "By that I mean that she used drugs, chiefly morphine, for nearly two years before she died. After the birth of her first child she was in a very serious condition, and it was then that the hypodermic needle became more constantly employed. I know from talking with her mother that she tried to stop the habit and would do so for weeks at a time, and then would come another period of ill health and the temptation to secure relief was too great to resist. At these times she would take morphine in large quantities and almost lived on it. She would go for days and days without food. She was half crazed and starved herself. I am convinced that it was in this condition that she destroyed herself. The drug helped the girl to a painless death."

Indicating this would be his line of defense, Haire said he had been contacted by an express agent at Murfreesboro, who said about a year ago he had expressed a five-pound package of morphine to Ocey Snead in New York. He had opened the case because of the mysterious woman in black who brought it in, and because of the high valuation she wanted placed on it.

The lawyer also recalled the accounts of the various doctors who had seen Ocey Snead under what they described as a dazed condition or a hypnotic spell. Most of the suicide notes were written while under the influence of morphine, said Haire.

As for his client, Mrs. Martin was sane. Fort's allegations were simply an attempt to shift responsibility onto her and thereby free his own clients, Miss Wardlaw and Mrs. Snead.

The conference with her new lawyer buoyed Mrs. Martin's spirits so substantially that she thanked the prison matron for being kind to her and intimated that she was about to be released.

"But I am not afraid of staying here in the Tombs," she declared. "I like it better here than my quarters just before coming here. I do not care for the grand jury or for the petit jury or the judge or the prosecutor. I do not even fear the electric chair. I would be glad to make a martyr of myself and take such a fate if I could help my kinswomen, who are guiltless as I. I could tell — tell a most astonishing story of our whole history. It will all be like the unfolding of the petals of a rose. I am innocent. I put my trust in God. I know that He will take care of me. I know that He also holds Prosecutor Mott right in the hollow of His hand and that no injustice will be done. The newspapers have relegated the troubles of my family to the back pages but I tell you they will soon be known through the front page once more."

Asked why, if all was so simple, she still withheld information, Mrs. Martin laughed heartily. "For my own vast amusement. I like to see the police hunt clues and make a great ado about them," she said, then caught herself and added quietly, "There has been a death in my family and I am not expected to feel gay."

Although she was content with her new lawyer, Mrs. Martin decided to take out added legal insurance. With her usual penchant for multiplicity she hired three additional advocates: Clark L. Jordan and George S. McDonald of 154 Nassau Street, and Samuel Fine of 309 Broadway, Manhattan.

23

ON MONDAY, DECEMBER 20, and Tuesday, December 21, Prosecutor Wilbur Mott presented his case to the grand jury of Essex County. The documentation, which had assumed the proportions of ancient Pelion heaped on Mount Ossa, was the first order of business, including the myriad suicide notes and the letters, never posted, of Ocey Snead to her husband Fletcher. On hand was an array of witnesses that included East Orange Police Chief James Bell, Sergeant William O'Neill, handwriting expert William Kinsley, Dr. William McKenzie, Charles Kirk and Edward Henry, the two East Orange boys who saw Mrs. Martin on November 29, druggist William Foster, trolley conductor George Handschuh, and a dozen more. Only half the witnesses had been called when the panel told the prosecutor it had come to a decision.

On Wednesday, December 22, the grand jury brought in two indictments against each of the three sisters. On the first count, all three were charged with murder in statutory form. On the second, all three were charged with aiding, counseling, and abetting Ocey Snead in self-murder. The bills were so drawn that any or all could be tried, each as principal, with the others as accessories, or, if the state chose to admit that Ocey Snead committed suicide, it could try any or all for murder in having aided and abetted her in self-destruction. Prosecutor Mott indicated he was inclined to try all three sisters together.

The fact that the indictments were so flexible seemed to indicate that the state, while showing reasonable grounds of guilt, had not established the exact nature of the crime.

Complying with his client's wishes, attorney Haire took out a writ of habeas corpus in the Supreme Court of New York and had it served on the keeper of the Tombs Prison. It was now incumbent on New Jersey to prove that Mrs. Martin was in that state when the crime was committed. This attempt to keep the elder sister in New York failed, witnesses having established that she was in New Jersey on November 29. Mrs. Martin had also failed in her efforts to get Mary Snead to join her in fighting extradition, and a heated quarrel between the two ensued.

Legal steps were delayed somewhat by the governors of the two states involved. Charles Evans Hughes of New York was absent from Albany over the Christmas season, and John Franklin Fort, the governor of New Jersey, was also out of his capital vacationing at Lakewood. Not until Tuesday, December 28, did Hughes honor the extradition papers signed the day before by Governor Fort.

The following day Mary Snead willingly signed the affidavit which acknowledged that she was the person named in the papers. Mrs. Martin put up a five-minute battle with counsel Samuel Fine. Only after being assured that Hughes's signature was genuine did she agree to write out her name.

Flanked by detectives, the two sisters were taken from New York State's jurisdiction and delivered into the hands of authorities in New Jersey. On arrival at the Essex County Jail in Newark they were allowed a pathetic ten-minute reunion with their sister Virginia before being assigned to adjoining cells. If the squat, two-story structure had elements which seemed familiar, it was because it was the work of John Haviland, a leading architect who had also designed the Tombs Prison in New York. For the trio, everything apparently came in duplicate and triplicate patterns, even prisons.

As Mrs. Martin settled down to her favorite occupation, newspaper reading, life played a second and a third satirical twist on her. In a news item, Mrs. Russell Sage, whom the sisters had several times solicited for funds, said she was offering Yale University $650,000 and the American Bible Society $500,000 if they could raise a matching sum on their own. In a full-page advertisement, the New York Life Insurance Company gave details of its sixty-fifth annual report. Total income for the last fiscal year was listed at $111,025,-342; total assets at $599,708,286; and total paid-for insurance in force at $2,002,809,227. It was New York Life which had refused to honor Ocey Snead's policies even to the extent of paying her burial expenses. They had amounted to $125.

24

"Jersey justice will be swift," Prosecutor Mott said at the time of the grand jury's indictments. His forecast was far off the mark. It was a month before the prisoners were even arraigned. On January 29, 1910, they made their first joint appearance before the court of oyer and terminer in Newark. Petite, self-effacing Mary Snead entered the jammed courtroom first, followed by the aquiline, aristocratic Virginia Wardlaw, and backed up by the always impressive, dynamic Caroline Martin, whose slight limp did not detract from her aura of will and power. At the railing the women in black sat side by side, like the three Fates watching the thread of life spinning itself out.

So important did Prosecutor Mott consider the case that he had asked William Gummere, chief justice of the New Jersey Supreme Court, to be the presiding officer. The distinguished jurist, whose name was pronounced in three syllables, Gum-me-re, accepted. From friends and relatives in the South had come funds to help in the defense of the prisoners. As a result, their legal forces had been increased. Franklin Fort continued to lead the team, his closest rapport being with Virginia Wardlaw. Samuel and Abner Kalish had been engaged to concentrate on Mary Snead, and Chandler W. Riker to focus his efforts on Caroline Martin.

It was Riker who opened proceedings by filing demurrers to the count of the indictment which charged the prisoners with being accessories to suicide. Under the laws of New Jersey, Riker contended, an accessory to suicide was guilty of nothing. Rather than debate this point, Prosecutor Mott said he would drop this allegation and proceed with the charge of murder. Accordingly, he had the clerk read that awesomely worded indictment which accused Caroline Martin and Virginia Wardlaw directly of killing Ocey Snead, and Mary Snead of being a part to the murder conspiracy.

". . . and that the said Caroline B. Martin and Virginia O. Wardlaw then and there, feloniously, deliberately, premeditatedly and of malice aforethought did take the said Ocey Wardlaw Martin Snead into both the hands of them, the said Caroline B. Martin and Virginia O. Wardlaw did then and there, feloniously, willfully, deliberately, premeditatedly, and of their malice aforethought, cast, throw, and push the said Ocey Wardlaw Martin Snead into a certain bathtub, there situated, wherein there was a great quantity of water, by means of which said casting, throwing, and pushing of the said Ocey Wardlaw Martin Snead into the bathtub aforesaid the said Ocey Wardlaw Martin Snead was then and there choked, suffocated, and drowned, and then and there instantly died.

"And that Mary Wardlaw Snead, of the city aforesaid, in the county aforesaid, before the felony and murder aforesaid by the aforesaid Caroline B. Martin and Virginia O. Wardlaw, did feloniously, maliciously, willfully, deliberately, premeditatedly, and of her malice aforethought, incite, move, procure, aid, abet, counsel, and recommend the said Caroline B. Martin and Virginia O. Wardlaw to do and commit the felony and murder aforesaid."

At the end of the reading, Chief Justice Gummere asked each of the sisters how they pleaded. "Not guilty," said Virginia Wardlaw in a soft low tone. "Not guilty," said Mary Snead, her voice scarcely audible. Struggling to her feet when called, Caroline Martin answered in strong, firm syllables, "I am absolutely not guilty. She was my only daughter."

The presiding judge set the trial date for April 11. The prisoners were led outside not to the customary Black Maria, but to a wagonette with glass windows extending along the sides. Through these they peered at the curious who had come to stare at them, then fell into conversation among themselves as they were driven away.

25

THE ILL FORTUNE WHICH SEEMED SO INEXTRICABLY BOUND up with the lives of the Wardlaw clan pursued the family even as the three sisters languished in jail. On February 6, their aunt, Mrs. Ocey Pollock, died in Christiansburg, Virginia. From her prison cell, Mrs. Martin sent out an obituary of the aged woman who had often helped the sisters, who had turned over Montgomery College to them, only to see it collapse and close.

"She died from a broken heart," wrote Mrs. Martin, "caused by the shock, surprise, and grief brought by the false accusations against her beloved nieces, the mother and aunts of Mrs. Ocey Snead. Mrs. Ocey Snead and Miss Virginia Oceana Wardlaw were both named after Mrs. Pollock, who had trained in Christian character and high integrity her beloved nieces, the mother and aunts of the lovely and lamented Ocey Snead. Miss Wardlaw, Mrs. Martin, and Mrs. Snead are suffering greatly from the bereavement of these two recent deaths in their family."

In her obituary, Mrs. Martin neglected to mention that the deceased was ninety-three years old.

Depression and suffering were in the air as the April 11 trial date neared. Early in the month, Virginia Wardlaw fell ill, plagued by intestinal disorders, and the trial was postponed. Mrs. Martin, under the strain of imprisonment, grew increasingly irascible and several times quarreled with Mary Snead. Each altercation was quickly smoothed over, however, for the elder sister sent daily letters to prominent people asking for their help, and in this correspondence Mary was her pliant amanuensis. No signature appeared on any of the outgoing documents other than the general one, "The Wardlaw Sisters."

In mid-May an intimation reached Warden Richard McGuinness that the three prisoners had entered into a suicide pact. Because Mrs. Martin was considered to exert a dominating influence, she was removed to new quarters on another tier, over her vigorous protests. Her sisters remained in adjoining cells. All opened onto a common court.

"I used my own judgment in separating Mrs. Snead and Miss Wardlaw from Mrs. Martin," said the warden. "I did not consult Prosecutor Mott or the counsel for the prisoners. I am responsible for the safety of the women and I propose, unless some natural causes intervene, to produce them in court."

Once again, however, the trial was postponed when a key prosecution witness, Detective William O'Neill, fell ill with scarlet fever.

Another severe setback for the sisters came in June. Their mother, Martha Eliza Wardlaw, died in a Manhattan hospital. And in late July, still another blow rained down on the sad trio. David Pollock Snead, the infant son of Ocey Snead, died at St. Christopher's Hospital in Brooklyn. Ill since birth, he had narrowly escaped with his life some time before when a fire swept through the hospital building.

The long hot summer was taking a pitiful toll of the Wardlaw clan. Sallow-faced, the sisters sat in their cells, read the newspapers, wrote their pleading letters, ate the austere, tasteless meals which were brought to them. One of the guards noted that they kept food twenty-four hours before eating it, regularly maintaining this day's interval. Often stale food was thrown out, for Caroline Martin and Virginia Wardlaw took only dishes easy to masticate, their sunken cheeks betraying the absence of almost all teeth.

As August began, the vacationing Prosecutor Mott suffered a sunstroke at Nantucket Beach and the trial was again postponed. One of the sisters would in any event have forced another delay. In her prison cell, Virginia Wardlaw lay desperately ill; her decline was so alarming that prison officials became suspicious.

Guards, under instructions to watch her closely, made a grim discovery. Sometimes she would give parts of her scant food away surreptitiously to other prisoners. On other occasions she would hide it in her cell until an opportune moment allowed her to toss scraps out of the window. Each day she was eating a little less. Virginia Wardlaw was slowly, methodically starving herself to death.

Thinking that perhaps the anxiety of prison life had caused a breakdown, jail physician Oswald Roth prescribed tonics. Warden McGuinness made up his mind that the sick woman would not be allowed to die because her stomach was unable to bear coarse prison fare. From his own table he and his wife sent delicacies. If Virginia Wardlaw had indeed been committing suicide by denying herself food, the body's fierce desire was now too strong for the mind's tragic resolve. Her nerve broke. She ate eagerly the food of refinement to which she had once been accustomed. Buttermilk was an especial favorite. Her condition improved.

On the third night, however, she looked at the tempting dishes without tasting them. Pretending she would eat later, she pushed them aside. Later she gave them to fellow prisoners, cautioning them to secrecy. Gaunt to begin with, she now grew skeletal, her skin tightly drawn over once graceful features, her eyes feverish and bright. From morning until night, she lay on her cot, scarcely moving, staring up at the ceiling.

She asked a lawyer, Jacob L. Newman, to be summoned, and told him, "I feel badly, very badly. I know I am going to die. I simply cannot stand this place. I want to die. I will never have to stand trial." Several times she started dictating her will, but each time hesitations about what to bequeath to whom made her stop.

Mrs. Martin was allowed into the cell during Newman's visit. At one point she placed her arms around her sister's neck and whispered into her ear. A change came over Virginia Wardlaw. Breaking the embrace she cried, "Leave me alone. Leave me alone, I tell you. You are driving me mad. Oh, I shall go mad." When she was unable to come to a decision about the will, the lawyer left.

"Just think," said Mrs. Martin as she too departed. "Three daughters of a clergyman spending eight months in a place like this, confined among people of this class."

As the sick woman's condition grew worse, Dr. Roth called in two other state physicians, Dr. Walter S. Washington and Dr. J. Henry Clark. After examining the patient they found she was suffering from serious intestinal trouble brought on by the inactive prison life and starvation. Although acknowledging that she was in great pain, Virginia Wardlaw made no complaint except to say she was weary and wished to rest.

On Monday, August 8, Chief Justice Gummere signed an order removing the prisoner from her jail cell to more hospitable quarters in the nearby house of detention. In a large airy room with six windows, two trained nurses stayed with her constantly. She feebly rejected attempts to give her nourishment. Finally, force feeding was resorted to. The physicians also administered heart stimulants and oxygen.

On Tuesday afternoon, August 9, she sank into torpitude and relatives were sent for. The youngest sister of the Wardlaw clan, Mrs. Bessie Spindle, arrived in Newark early Thursday morning. At noon a younger brother, the Reverend Albert G. Wardlaw, joined her, having recently given up his parish in South Carolina to devote full time to helping his sisters. Accompanying the clergyman was Judge Archer A. Phlegar, a family friend and counsellor.

All three hurried to the bedside, where the patient's breath came in short gasps. She had been comatose for the last thirty-six hours. They remained until 1 P.M., then went out for lunch. Afterwards, Bessie Spindle and Judge Phlegar went on to attend to some business. The brother returned to the bedside, where he was joined by Chauncey Havens Beasley, a new counsel aiding in the defense of the sisters.

At two thirty Dr. Roth announced that the patient, whose pulse was barely perceptible, had little more than an hour to live. The lawyer went immediately to inform Mary Snead and Caroline Martin. The two sisters, in deepest grief, asked permission to say farewell to the dying woman. Undersheriff Reilly, temporarily in charge, said that he feared the visit of the two might precipitate death. He would not allow it without the presence of a physician in the room. Since Dr. Roth had left to attend to other patients, attendants went to search for him.

Beasley returned to the room. On either side of the cot a nurse sat silently, observing the faded form of a woman who had once represented the culture and dignity of a proud society. When the Reverend Wardlaw, his eyes filling involuntarily with tears, sank to his knees in prayer, the lawyer and nurses also kneeled. For one brief second, Virginia Wardlaw stirred. Her brother felt a slight pressure of the hand as if in recognition. This was followed by a deep-drawn sigh, and then her spirit fluttered away, leaving behind a smile on lips that had grown almost white. Bessie Spindle and Judge Phlegar returned an hour after the end came. The efforts to locate Dr. Roth were also tardy, and Caroline Martin and Mary Snead were denied the opportunity to say good-bye.

An autopsy by Dr. William McKenzie showed pulmonary edema, resulting in congestion of the lungs, as the direct cause of death. It was starvation, however, which had produced a physical decline, the atrophy of organs, and the consequent congestion. In the physician's view, the patient was at first able to eat, but did not. Later, her general physical condition resulted in a loss of appetite. Near the end, her stomach was in such a state of deterioration that digestion was no longer possible.

East Orange undertaker W. N. Knapp was engaged to prepare the body. Despite many requests to view the remains, the family would allow no display. On Saturday evening the brother and sister and Judge Phlegar accompanied the coffin to the Market Street station of the Pennsylvania Railroad. The next morning they arrived in Christiansburg, where the body was taken to the Methodist Church. On Monday, August 15, the Reverend Van Horn conducted a simple funeral service attended by a small assembly of relatives and friends. Afterwards the body was laid to rest in the local cemetery, almost in the shade of the huge firs and elms which surrounded Montgomery College. There, for a little while at least, Virginia Wardlaw had known happiness.

What secrets did she carry with her to the grave? Was her slow, self-inflicted torture induced simply by the intolerableness of prison life, or did she have a deeper motive, a fierce determination to avoid by any means giving testimony that might harm her sisters? Those sisters had asked to see her. If they knew they were guilty, they evidently did not fear that at the end she might weaken and with dying lips speak words that would condemn them.

26

DEATH HAD REMOVED THE ONE PERSON who admitted being in the house when Ocey Snead lay dying. There was speculation that the state might drop charges against the two remaining sisters. The prosecution quickly dispelled these rumors. Its case was weakened, admitted Wilbur Mott, but he would try Mary Snead and Caroline Martin in September. Almost unbelievably, another delay ensued when one of the attorneys for the defense, Chandler Riker, was stricken ill.

To her team of counsellors Mrs. Martin proclaimed, "I am being driven crazy in this place. When am I going to get out of here? I cannot stand it much longer."

The hapless prisoner was unaware of the full irony in her remarks. On September 24, Adrian Riker, on behalf of Mrs. Bessie Spindle and the Reverend Albert G. Wardlaw, took action to have her declared insane. To add even further to fate's mischievousness, it was Mrs. Martin's sixty-fifth birthday.

In support of their contention, lawyers secured affidavits from Dr. Walter Washington and Dr. Harry A. Cotton, who reported on their examinations of Mrs. Martin over a period of time and certified that the prisoner was not in a fit mental condition to be placed on trial but should be placed in isolation. Their statements were submitted to the court of common pleas, which granted the request for an inquiry. The court thereupon appointed three physicians to examine Mrs. Martin for the state, Dr. J. Henry Clark, Dr. Christopher C. Beling, and Police Surgeon William H. Hicks. Louis Hood, a special counsel for the state, was named to work with Prosecutor Wilbur Mott. The prisoner was to be represented by a team that included the law firm of Riker and Riker, Samuel Kalish, and Chauncey Havens Beasley, himself a former judge. Judge Jay Ten Eyck, in the discretion given him by the law, elected to hear the case without a jury. The site for the inquiry was Essex County's court of oyer and terminer, in Newark's Hall of Records.

Once again, on Wednesday, November 2, the doughty Mrs. Martin was led into a courtroom on the arms of detectives. Over her large square shoulders flowed a black cape which reached to the floor, seeming even to have the extra length of a train. From a round widow's bonnet hung a double black veil, almost impenetrable, extending far down the length of her body.

At the court rail she took her seat, motionless for the moment, her black gloved hands intertwined. Clearly her position was not an enviable one. If judged insane, she would be sent to an asylum. If judged sane, she would have to stand trial for murder. Toward the lawyers trying to prove her mad she displayed an understandable ambivalence. These men flanked her on either side. Seated among the spectators were her brother and sister who had brought about the hearing. The Reverend Albert Wardlaw was a bald, round-faced, somber man, and Mrs. Bessie G. Spindle was clearly a gentlewoman, with soft, warm features.

Judge Ten Eyck explained that the hearing was strictly a special statutory proceeding to spare the accused a trial if found insane. For the defense, Adrian Riker said he would bring forth five experts and nine other witnesses.

"Here is a woman charged in an indictment with having

murdered her own daughter," he said to the court, "and if she is insane she should not be brought to trial. We will show by witnesses that Mrs. Martin had mental peculiarities even as a child and that they have continued with her."

As the first defense witness, Judge Archer Phlegar of Christiansburg took the stand. Speaking with a pronounced Southern drawl, the family solicitor said he had known the prisoner for forty years, from before her marriage, and intimately since 1884 when he started acting as her counsel. Throughout the years she had been difficult and troublesome, always "tinkering" with titles to her property. Five years ago, because of her bad business judgment, her unusually high self-regard, and her disregard of the amenities, Judge Phlegar had dropped her account.

"She was most pertinacious, suh," Phlegar testified, "and when she made up her mind to have her own way, it was a caution."

In early November 1909, Mrs. Martin had begged him to resume handling her affairs. She made her appeal with tearful insistence but he had refused. She appeared to him to be failing fast. After her arrest on December 15, 1909, he had talked to Bessie Spindle. The two had contacted Virginia Wardlaw. All agreed that Ocey Snead's insurance policies should be reassigned to the judge, the money to be placed in trust as a defense fund for the sisters.

In January of 1910 Phlegar had gone for the first time to see Mrs. Martin in prison. Earlier he had thought her mind affected, but now he was more convinced than ever.

"What was your reception?" the defense counsel asked.

"She gave me a frigid bow and after a delay she shook hands."

"And then?"

"It was hard for me to understand, suh, how a woman who had been raised like Mrs. Mawhtain could act the way she did. She was in a rage almost the entire time I was there. I never saw a woman of her culture in such a mood."

The source of Mrs. Martin's dissatisfaction, said Phlegar, was the defense fund. She was afraid the money would be wasted and denounced all concerned with the reassignment of the insurance policies. The judge she called an "archtraitor." Franklin Fort, her lawyer at the time, also came in for healthy abuse, in part because of his Republican political affiliations. A Democratic lawyer must be employed, Mrs. Martin said, to offset any advantage Prosecutor Mott might have through his "black-hearted Republican" associations.

The first interview with Phlegar lasted six hours. At a second, Mrs. Martin refused to give him information he needed to use in her defense, and a third saw her upbraiding him as a deceiver and squanderer of the defense fund.

When the Southern jurist had completed his testimony, special state counsel Louis Hood asked him to produce any letters that the prisoner had sent him from jail.

"I have never written any letters to him — never in my life!" Mrs. Martin cried excitedly.

As a constable hurried to quiet her down, Hood explained that he meant letters sent from the jail which had to do with employing counsel for the sisters. These letters were signed, "The Wardlaw Sisters." After the documents in question were introduced into the evidence, Adrian Riker asked a crucial question.

"In your opinion, is Mrs. Martin capable of giving the necessary aid that she should give for the preparation of her defense?"

"I have no hesitation in saying that she has not any real comprehension of her situation and what may be her end," said Phlegar, and left the stand.

A second witness from the South, Mrs. Laura Jones, told the court in detail of Mrs. Martin's eccentricities. The seamstress wife of a Christiansburg livery stable manager, she had known the prisoner over a three-year period and done sewing for her during 1908.

"I used to make her a waist," she testified, "and she would give me the money and say, 'Go get me the goods and make me another one.' Once she ordered three waists and put them all on at the same time, one over the other. She would never allow buttons or hooks to be fixed to them."

"Well, didn't she ever carry anything in her hand?"

"Oh, yes, she almost always carried a small handbag. She would carry it slipped up on her arm. Once though when she was holding on to her skirt it threatened to slip off. She just shoved me away and told me to mind my own business when I offered to help her."

"What did you see?"

"Just plain naked hide."

"What other dealings did you have with Mrs. Martin?"

"For three weeks I gathered old clothing for her and she paid me a good price."

"What did she want of that clothing?"

"She said she wanted to give it to the families of poor preachers so their children could go to school. Another time she offered me double rates for magazines, books, and old newspapers. She said these were for the amusement of the children of her boarders."

"Did you provide them?"

"I did."

"And what else?"

"Once she offered me five dollars for a couple of kittens."

"You took them?"

"I did."

"You did swindle her, didn't you?"

"Well, I guess I did. I took what she offered."

As the first day's proceedings came to an end, Mrs. Martin, who had displayed only a perfunctory interest, got up and slowly walked out, escorted by a bailiff.

The prisoner appeared far more attentive at the second session, on Thursday morning, leaning forward at the rail and peering intently at Ritta Sublit as the latter took the stand. A Negro maid, the witness said that she was in Mrs. Martin's employ at Soule College during 1903 and 1904. She first thought her employer strange when she insisted on giving her thirty dollars a month for services customarily paid for at the rate of two dollars a week. Next she saw that Mrs. Martin had the habit of packing newspapers and trash away in boxes. Soon there were many other evidences of unusual behavior.

"I was supposed to dress her but she wouldn't let me," the maid began, giving a description of her duties. "There were times when she wouldn't let me come near her. She was powerful queer about her clothes. She would wear a night-gown all day except when she went out, and then she would put on an old black skirt and waist without anything under them. Sometimes she would go without any stockings and sometimes with only one. She would go three or four weeks without change of clothing. She would stay in bed for weeks at a time, her hair hanging down wild and loose. She didn't take care of her hair nor her body. I don't remember her ever using the bathtub. She wouldn't even let me change the bedclothes except when she went away."

"When she stayed in bed, did she take any medicine or see a doctor?"

"No, sir."

"Were you also supposed to care for Mrs. Martin's room?"

"Her room was the nastiest thing I ever saw. She never let me clean it the two years I was there, although that was what I was hired for. All over the floor was food and coal and ashes. She would never let me take any food away from her room after I had brought it, but it would stay there until it rotted. I would bring her a tray and she would only touch the coffee, so I would watch my time and steal the rest away. And she never would let me sweep."

"What would happen if you did sweep or take away food and Mrs. Martin saw you?"

"She'd get powerful mad."

"Do you remember any other habits of hers?"

"She kept a big box of money in her room and would scatter the five and ten dollar bills about on the floor just for the pleasure of throwing the money."

"Did you pick them up?"

"When I picked them up she threw them right back down."

"Were there any other situations involving money?"

"One time Mrs. Martin sent me to buy her a ten-cent comb and gave me a ten dollar bill. I brought her the comb, and Mrs. Martin says, 'Take that money and go and buy me ten dollars' worth of combs.'"

"Did you buy the combs?"

"Yes, sir. And one time she took my apron and tied it on herself as she lay in bed. 'Take a ten dollar bill,' she said, 'and go buy a heap of aprons.'"

"Did you sleep at the college or go home for the night?"

"Sometimes Mrs. Martin insisted I stay over. She'd give my husband a dollar for letting me stay. And she'd give me a dollar, too. I'd sleep in a cot near her bed. Mrs. Martin kept a double-barreled shotgun right at the head of her bed."

"Did you ever see her handle the gun?"

"One night I was awakened about one o'clock by a shot. I jumped from the bed and saw Mrs. Martin sitting on the cot laughing, with the gun between her knees. 'What are you doing, Mrs. Martin?' I asked. 'Why, Ritta, if that gun had gone off you would have been a rich woman,' she said. I didn't know what she meant, but I took the gun away from her and locked it up. She didn't seem to think that the gun had been fired off, but it had. The shot went into the ceiling."

The next witness, Miss Mary E. Van Wagenen, was currently a resident of Chicago. From 1903 to 1905 she had taught vocal music and expression at Soule College. Her memory of Mrs. Martin was of a woman strange at all times, never normal in anything, one who often went on journeys from which she returned in the dead of night; she would shut herself up for weeks on end and invest even the most trivial affairs with needless mystery.

"She was erratic, vague in her business plans, changeable in mood and desire, and sudden in her demands so that I had no confidence in her words or actions," said Miss Van Wagenen. "She would be either wildly exhilarated or very much depressed, morose or talkative. At one commencement I remember her talking in such a disconnected manner that I fairly made up my mind she was not in her right senses."

"Can you tell us what sort of thing would raise or lower her spirits?"

"When speaking of her wishes to extend the college — just wild, unfounded schemes — she would be terribly excited. The definite things that depressed her were the insignificant faults of Ocey, who was a student at the college. She was very exacting with her. When she asked me to take charge of her education, she gave the impression the girl would have plenty of money when she was twenty-one. Ocey didn't proceed very far because the mother was always interfering. When Ocey was away visiting relatives, I saw Mrs. Martin receive a letter from her. She seemed to have a peculiar aversion to it. On the other hand, once her daughter sang an insignificant song in a very poor manner. Mrs. Martin was exhilarated as if the child was something great. But Mrs.

Martin did not need occasions to produce her moods. For no particular reason she could become gloomy and low-spirited."

"Did you see Mrs. Martin outside of the school environment?

"Occasionally we dined together."

"What was her attitude at table?"

"She ate little and that seemingly under protest. She was nervous and restless and constantly wriggled her hands. She would take up her knife and fork and drop them again, and always she was ill at ease."

"Was she critical of any other persons than her daughter?"

"She was always hard to please, always dissatisfied, with a violent temper. She had an exaggerated opinion of her own importance and achievements. She thought of herself as a person of great power and influence."

"Do you remember any particular incidents that occurred during the years you taught at Soule?"

"Once Miss Wardlaw was caught in a folding bed. She came staggering into my room and fell in a dead faint. A doctor was hastily called and while we were working we heard a piercing scream from below, from Mrs. Martin, who had stepped on a pin. She came into my room and crouched down. All the time we were working over Miss Wardlaw she laughed excitedly and told funny stories until we were sure she was quite mad."

"What was her attitude toward money?"

"She could be very lavish. She offered me a hundred fifty dollars a month to educate Ocey, much too much for the services needed. We reduced this to fifty dollars a month. When buying dresses for Ocey she would not buy one of a kind, but duplicate dresses."

At the end of this second day's session, Mrs. Martin made her exit as before, only to veer suddenly into the judge's pri-

vate chambers. Constable Philip McManus, only a step behind, quickly retrieved her and led her outside.

Court did not reconvene until Monday, November 7,
1910, when bank president Jack L. Vaughan of Redford,
Virginia, recounted at length the many occasions on which
he had encountered Mrs. Martin. The prisoner, he said,
made so many overtures for raising money that he could not
recall them all, outlined more financial schemes than any
person he had ever met. At times her business acumen
seemed to him to be sharp, but then again it would become
disjointed. As for her personal habits and appearance, they
seemed most peculiar. On one occasion as she was getting
into a carriage, Vaughan noted that one of her feet was bare.

"I never said a thing he is telling," interjected Mrs. Martin,
visibly exasperated. "I am no more insane than anybody
else. I am not insane and I desire counsel. I don't want to be
tried in this court anyway. I can't get a fair trial. The lawyers represent Mrs. Spindle and Mr. Wardlaw and there is
no one here for me. I understand that the prosecutor is to
prosecute me if I am guilty and to protect me if I am innocent. Why can't the prosecutor try this case? I am not guilty
and I want a lawyer . . ."

As the outburst continued, Judge Ten Eyck pounded his
gavel for order. When the prisoner went on, he adjourned
the court for the day.

By the time the hearing resumed on the following Tuesday, Mrs. Martin had regained her composure. The next two
witnesses were calculated to shatter it. Her brother, the Reverend Albert Wardlaw, testified that in the family background there were several case histories of mental imbalance, and that Caroline Martin's life had followed a pattern
of gradual impairment of the faculties.

"In her girlhood she was neat and pretty, of sparkling eye
and great intellectuality," said her brother. "She was always

dressed in keeping with the means of her father, a minister. I think she was recognized as a girl of unusual mentality. She began teaching at home at thirteen, and at fifteen or sixteen in public schools, pupils much older than herself."

"Were you ever at any time under her personal control and guidance?"

"She directed both my school and daily life in New York."

"Can you give us your impressions of your sister between 1884 and 1892?"

"Her dress and manner became unusual. In 1891, she suggested a family reunion, where her conduct and remarks were very strange. She said she was the equal of her Creator and called herself Salvatore. She had a great air of superiority.

"I took one trip with her to Europe, where I was to enter school. In London she lost a pocketbook containing a thousand dollars. I found it in the railroad station. In Switzerland she unaccountably left me at the school with only four dollars and my father had to send money so I could live. In 1892 an uncle gave me some money for the education of my sister Bessie. My aunt wanted to borrow it and was very angry when I refused to give it to her. After a time I went to Princeton to study for the ministry and it was many years before I saw Caroline again."

Wednesday's key witness was Mrs. Bessie Spindle, more than twenty years younger but bearing a marked resemblance to the prisoner. She corroborated her brother's story of Caroline Martin's precocious childhood and later mental decline. She also elicited a firm protest from the main object of her recital.

"She was about twenty-six when I first remember her," said Mrs. Spindle, "a slender young woman with compelling eyes and a strong resolute mouth. She had the most beautiful hair I have ever seen and everyone spoke of her lovely hands. She was teaching in fashionable boarding schools in New York and making a great deal of money. She spent it lavishly, staying at expensive hotels and wearing fine clothes. One Christmas when she heard me say I wanted a workbox, she sent me seven or eight."

In 1880 the witness had gone to Christiansburg to visit her aunt, Mrs. Ocey Pollock. Also present were her brother John, the Princetonian, her mother and father, and her older sister Caroline. Trouble was apparently in the air, and there were "some terrible scenes" in which Bessie did not participate. Mrs. Pollock walked the floor all one night, while Caroline sat weeping and wringing her hands. Her father's death was hastened by these scenes, Bessie Spindle felt. She was never able to find out what caused the intense family anguish.

Five years later, Bessie and her mother went to New York to visit Caroline, then living in a house at 37 East 39th Street for which she was paying three hundred dollars a month rent.

"Caroline was greatly changed and had begun to neglect herself," said Bessie. "In the schoolroom her manner was of exalted enthusiasm, but when she came home she would collapse. Often she went out on snowy days without underclothing, and it was not because she did not have money, because she was supposed to be making eight or ten thousand dollars a year teaching in the public schools, running a school of her own, and also a boardinghouse. Her manner was extremely irritable and dominant. She demanded implicit obedience and declared that her judgment was infallible. On one occasion she became annoyed over some slight thing her sister Mary had done and slapped her. When I remonstrated with her for her appearance, she said the trials of rearing a family were so great she had no time to dress. She likened herself to Christ in her suffering."

Within the same year, 1885, Bessie Wardlaw became Mrs.

Richard Spindle. Her sister Caroline came South for the ceremony. While the money for Bessie's education had been withheld from the demanding Caroline by Albert, Bessie on her own had turned part of it over to her as a loan. On the wedding morning, Caroline asked her to sign a release for it. When Bessie refused, a violent scene followed, with Caroline crying that the money belonged to her by divine right of creatorship, just as, in fact, everything in the family belonged to her. Bessie unwillingly signed the release.

The sisters saw little of one another until 1902, when Caroline Martin reappeared at the Spindle home in Christiansburg. On the pretext of consulting Richard Spindle on business matters she asked to stay the night. At the end of seven months, however, she was still encamped in the house, more and more domineering, her untidy room littered with an accumulation of debris, including food morsels she would not allow to be removed. Finally, Bessie Spindle asked her to end her visit. The request aroused Mrs. Martin's ire. She flatly refused to leave. The books in the house, the pictures, the gifts from friends were all really hers, she insisted, for the Spindles would never have had the friends to give them if it had not been for her.

"She said she had raised the family to the level upon which it stood," said the witness, "that she had made terrible sacrifices for it, that she was the sole arbiter of its destinies, and that my very hope of heaven rested in her. She said if her directions had been followed, we would never have had any troubles, failures, or misfortunes, but that we would be worth millions."

"Did you support her during this period?"

"When she came she had not one change of clothing. I gave her wearing apparel. Once she offered me ten dollars for a dressing sacque that wasn't worth more than a dollar and a half. She had plenty of money, carried it carelessly

and spent it foolishly. The children found five and ten dollar
bills all over the house."

"Was Ocey with her?"

"After several months, she sent for her. I was running a
private school and Caroline wanted Ocey to help in the
school. One day she dressed the child in one of her own
skirts and put up her hair in outlandish shape. When I protested she said she wanted the child, if she was to teach, to
look as old as possible. She herself attempted to teach but
the effect was disorganizing. She insisted on making the
children romp and offered them twenty-five cents each to
get their lessons."

At this time, Bessie Spindle said, she had contemplated
having her sister put into an asylum. She wrote her brother
Albert, then assigned to a parish in South Carolina. He replied that he could not leave his work at the moment and
suggested she see a lawyer. Unwilling to proceed alone, she
contacted her sister Virginia, who came and took the unin-
vited guest away. Empty-handed on arrival, Caroline Martin
left with seven large trunks filled principally with old newspapers.

"She has made frantic appeals to me for help in this case,"
said Bessie Spindle, bringing her account up to date. "She
begged me to get witnesses for her. She wanted me to appeal to Mrs. Russell Sage, Helen Gould, and Mrs. Burton
Harrison. The electric switch guard over the settee in the
jail's visitor's room, she says, is a sounding board connected
with tubes so that detectives on the other side can hear all
that is said. She believes the other inmates of the jail are
paid to spy on her. She says it is impossible for her to get
justice here, that Mr. Mott is to get a hundred thousand dollars from the legislature for his work in the case, that Mr.
Hood is to get fifty thousand dollars from the insurance
companies, and that her own lawyer, Mr. Fort, got his.

"Where do I come in?" defense counsel Riker asked.

"She says Mr. Riker can be bought but that he wants too much."

"That is not so," Mrs. Martin exclaimed as laughter echoed in the courtroom.

"Mrs. Martin," said Judge Ten Eyck, "you will have a chance to make a statement when your time comes."

"That was a privileged communication. I don't think this is fair to Mr. Mott or to me."

"You will have a chance to make a statement when your time comes," the judge repeated.

"That will soon be forgotten."

"No, it will not," said Ten Eyck, and adjourned for the day.

For a moment there was further gaiety in the room as several of the attorneys began to chat with one another.

"Is there anything amusing in this, when my life is at stake?" demanded Mrs. Martin.

"Your life is not at stake, and you are not the subject of this laughter," said Judge Ten Eyck.

Slowly the woman whom witnesses had described as slender and stylish in youth made her way down the aisle. Her shapeless mass of black swathed in veils formed a startling contrast to the touching evocations of yesteryear.

The last of the defense witnesses from the South took the stand on Thursday, November 10. Miss Nannie Ransom, a Negro, told of her experiences as Mrs. Martin's maid in Murfreesboro in 1904. She said that her employer spent much of her time in bed, tasted only a bit of food before hiding the rest in various places, including the bed, and was careless of her appearance. Only about once a month would she comb her hair. Whenever she struck a tangle, she would pin the hair up and wait several days before going on, said the witness. The maid also heard the family discuss sending Mrs.

Martin to a sanitarium. In fact, Mrs. Martin herself told her that her sisters wanted to send her away. No reason was given for the proposed action.

It was the life and behavior of Mrs. Martin in New York which next came under scrutiny, as lawyers Maxwell Elliott and Franklin Fort were called to testify. Elliott told of talks with the prisoner about her public school pension, on which he had advanced loans. To him she often appeared irrational. Recently he had seen her and found her strongly opposed to the reassignment of Ocey Snead's insurance policies. She wanted the money to go to her daughter's child rather than for a defense fund.

"Praise God for the truth, once!" interjected Mrs. Martin in a voice charged with emotion.

"She would not believe the little boy was dead," said Elliott.

"I don't now," said Mrs. Martin. "Mr. Mott has him somewhere. Mr. Mott has killed my grandchild and my sister."

The appearance of her earliest counsel, Franklin Fort, brought Mrs. Martin's violent temper and sharp mind into full focus. Her running commentary on his testimony and her constant interruptions were so disruptive that the hearing was several times halted. The display provoked considerable hilarity from courtroom spectators and stern warnings from Judge Ten Eyck.

Fort began with an account of his first meetings with the prisoner, his almost daily visits to the Tombs Prison in New York, where he was never able to get any meaningful plan of defense from her.

"She said that she was quite capable of preparing her own defense," he testified. "She wanted a corps of lawyers, among whom were to be Choate, Untermyer, and seven or eight other prominent New Yorkers. When I suggested the matter of compensation she said she could get thirty or forty thousand dollars from prominent people."

"Falsehood, sir. Please note an exception, sir," Mrs. Martin said, inaugurating her barrage of objections.

"She had a habit of carrying an enormous roll of valueless papers," Fort went on, "and she would point out cases in England where the law and facts were entirely different from her case, and state that should be her line of defense."

"Yes," said Mrs. Martin, "I showed you cases of disbarred lawyers who had cheated their clients."

"Please, Mrs. Martin," cautioned Judge Ten Eyck, but even he could not keep from smiling.

"Mrs. Martin was against my going South to see Judge Phlegar and members of her family who at one point wanted her put in an asylum."

"I never said a word against my family. Exception, please."

"I told her in discussing the chances of the case that if I had nothing more than she had been able to give me in forming a defense, a conviction would be certain."

"A lie. A lie. He never said a word to me about a conviction."

"I must ask you not to interrupt, Mrs. Martin."

"What does a youngster like him know of the workings of an old lady's mind?"

"I have tried to gain information from Mrs. Mary Snead and Miss Wardlaw, but Mrs. Martin would never let either of them speak to me while she was there."

"No, sir, I didn't, and for a good reason, and I now warn anyone against conversing with you unless they wish to be misrepresented afterwards."

"Please go on, Mr. Fort. Mrs. Martin, I must warn you again not to interrupt."

"But why do you let a man sit there and tell such lies? You'll take his word against the word of an old woman. I know you will."

"I'm obligated to hear every witness but not necessarily to believe everything I hear. Your rights will be protected. Mr. Fort, go on."

"When Mrs. Mary Snead did on occasion speak up, the prisoner would say, 'Shut up, you fool. You were always a fool.'"

"We don't use that expression in the South. That may be yours but it isn't ours."

"Mrs. Martin was under the impression that an article, or rather an obituary, she had written about an aunt who had died in the South would help her case immensely."

"You are misrepresenting a dead woman."

"It won't do you any good to keep up these interruptions."

"I don't expect any good in Essex County."

The continuing crossfire from the prisoner was clearly amusing the spectators. Judge Ten Eyck's gavel was used often to silence them, but now he had momentarily had enough. He declared an hour's recess. When court resumed, it appeared that the respite had served only to refresh Mrs. Martin, who swiftly renewed her assault. Even before Fort could continue she turned to Wilbur Mott and drew him into the arena.

"I don't want to go to any asylum," she said. "I call on you as prosecutor of Essex County to defend and protect me. I have no attorney and no way to help myself. It takes no end of money to employ attorneys in this town."

"Mrs. Martin, I implore you not to interrupt. This is a court of law. Mr. Fort, continue."

"On one occasion, a New York newspaper came to me and offered to pay five hundred dollars for an article on any subject by Miss Wardlaw. I conveyed the offer and it was rejected. From this, however, Mrs. Martin, who heard of the offer, got the idea that I was seeking statements from the sisters to aid in their prosecution."

"That's just what you were doing."

"She accused me of being in collusion with the prosecution, and all the judges of the county."

"Anyone who has been through the horrors of the Civil War, and has been searched and stripped for jewelry by brutal Union soldiers, knows that all black-hearted Republicans hang together. That is the reason I want a Democratic lawyer."

"Sit down, Mrs. Martin, or I will clear the courtroom," said Judge Ten Eyck, nearing the end of his patience. Reluctantly, the prisoner sank into her seat.

"Mrs. Martin said that all papers in the case, even personal letters addressed to me, belonged to her," the witness resumed. "She said if it hadn't been for her I would not have received them."

"Now tell the truth."

"Mr. Fort, can you sum up your overall impressions of your former client?"

"She impressed me as a woman wholly without feeling. Referring to her daughter Ocey Snead, she spoke of her only as the 'deceased,' never of her as a daughter."

"Lies! May God judge him for the lies he has told today."

"She always referred to the murder charge in a casual way, such as . . ."

"Is this a murder trial?" Mrs. Martin shouted, on her feet once more. "I beg the judge to intervene. This is not a murder hearing."

"Sit down, Mrs. Martin. No one said this was a murder hearing."

"Oh, well. The court is bought. The lawyers are bought, and I'll be electrocuted."

"You are not on trial for your life. For the last time, sit down."

"I'm not a crazy woman," the fulminating woman in black continued, ignoring the judge. "This man's testimony is a tissue of lies. They want to put me into an asylum but I don't want to go. I want somebody who can be near me and protect my rights. Mr. Fort has been quoting a dead woman, and that isn't according to law. I want somebody who can take my objections. I can't remember all the lies. How can this young fellow, with seven years' practice in the police courts, judge the mind of a woman?"

Unable to control the session, Judge Ten Eyck angrily gaveled the prisoner into silence and adjourned the hearing for a week's cooling-off period. Mrs. Martin left the room shouting a new series of protestations.

A melodramatic incident preceded her return to the limelight, providing her with dubious support. Just as the inquiry was about to reopen, on Thursday, November 17, a disheveled-looking man of about seventy walked into the courtroom. He sauntered up to Constable James Reid and asked if Mrs. Martin was in the room. When Reid pointed out the prisoner, the man handed him a faded bouquet of carnations and ferns.

"Please give these to Mrs. Martin," he said. "The delay in this case is a disgrace. If there was any such delay in the South as there has been in this state both the judge and the lawyers would be shot."

Constable Reid considered the man's manner suspicious. When he exclaimed he had been dead three times and come back to life each time, that he knew there was no hell but only a pit for the wicked, the constable and two associates hustled him out of the courtroom. In an office off the hallway, they found that he was carrying a fully loaded revolver in his hip pocket. The gun was confiscated. One of the constables recognized the man as Oliver B. Matthews, who had recently been paroled from the Overbrook Insane Asylum. He had had no intentions of using the revolver, said Matthews. He was simply concerned that a Southern gentlewoman, one of his compatriots, was forced to endure intolerable delays before being brought to trial. Detectives held him in custody pending an inquiry into his status.

Oblivious of this parenthetical interlude, Mrs. Martin unaccountably took a seat near a window, at a distance from her team of lawyers, and delivered a passionate soliloquy.

"I am here without a lawyer, a jury, a friend, or money," she intoned. "I am being crushed by the gigantic machine of men. Men, men, men! Can't I tell when they lie? There is no justice in Essex County. Why, if a girl takes a drink here when tired and hungry, she gets ninety days and the saloonkeeper rides in automobiles. I am falsely accused for the purpose of confiscating my property and for the glorification of the prosecution and the insurance companies. They have even hired persons to imitate my handwriting. I had a thousand dollars a year income. Why should I ruin sixty-five years of a good life by doing what they say I did?"

On entering, Judge Ten Eyck ordered her to take her seat. Samuel Kalish, associate counsel for the defense, took the stand. He testified to Mrs. Martin's peculiar behavior, her boasting about influential friends like Mrs. Russell Sage and Hetty Green, supposedly the wealthiest woman in the world, and to her rambling, disjointed conversation.

"When I sought information as to where she was and what she did with relation to Mrs. Snead, her daughter, she would say, 'You are not my counsel,' or, 'We cannot talk here. There are spies all around.' She said everyone was conspiring against her," Kalish recounted, "the governor, lawyers, the insurance companies, the prosecution. She insisted that if I could get her out long enough to see Mr. Mott, the prosecutor, she could raise fifty thousand dollars for the defense. I think she is insane and unable to prepare her defense."

After hearing this witness, Judge Ten Eyck called Mrs. Martin herself to the stand. Her response was the wildest outburst to date. She was a victim of conspiracy, she shouted, the court was bribed, and all efforts were being made to railroad her to prison. Absolutely refusing to be sworn, she began to upbraid the court so violently that her black bonnet fell off. The incident set off yet a new burst of temper. The woman who hitherto had refused to show her face ripped away the sheltering black veils and began marching up and down the aisle, ranting almost incoherently. Constable Carl Schneider tried to control her, but only elicited a protesting scream of rage. Using all his powers of persuasion, Judge Ten Eyck finally induced her to sit down, where she promptly started unlacing her shoes. The judge took a seat next to her and tried to calm her, all to no avail.

Finally he cleared the courtroom, allowing only lawyers and physicians involved in the case to remain. In a semisecret session he questioned the prisoner. Reporters out in the corridor could hear Mrs. Martin's strident voice berating everyone near her. A recess was called, after which she started a new tirade. The exhausted judge adjourned the court.

Postponing the prisoner's own reappearance on the stand, Ten Eyck scheduled a parade of medical experts, beginning with three for the defense, Dr. Walter Washington, Dr. William Mabon, and Dr. Harry Cotton.

Dr. Cotton, medical director of the State Hospital for the Insane at Trenton, spent an entire day telling of his analysis of the prisoner's mind. Three times Mrs. Martin burst in on his testimony, which detailed her alleged insanity.

Dr. Cotton began by citing the "neurotic" family stock,

the evidence of insanity on the mother's side which he said
predisposed the daughter to a similar impairment. He told
of her early reading ability, her precocity at the age of three,
her youth of extreme attractiveness and intellectuality, the
middle years of growing eccentricity and irritability, and the
later manifestations of contempt for manners and conven-
tionality.

In his interviews with her he had seen clear evidence of
two aspects of insanity which he classified as chronic delusional and pre-senile delusional. These were characterized
by exaggerated egotism, emotional irritability, impairment
of judgment, and delusions of persecution.

On one occasion she had told him of the "treachery" of
Franklin Fort who had sold her out for five hundred dollars
and who had killed her sister Virginia. She also confided that
she suspected Virginia of being insane. Another time she
complained bitterly when the warden removed papers from
her cell, a massive accumulation weighing more than eight
hundred pounds. Oft repeated were her accounts of persecution by Wilbur Mott, by Governor Hughes of New York,
whom she considered the lackey of the insurance companies,
and by the police. In prison she told of being hounded by a
spy system, with a girl prisoner as chief agent. Most of the
time she had no real use or need for friends, she told Cotton.
All her life she had wished to be alone.

Suspicions do not denote insanity until without reason and
fact they harden into morbid fixed beliefs, said Dr. Cotton.
With Mrs. Martin, this hardening seemed to have taken
place very gradually; the year 1902 marked a turning point
where suspicions had developed into delusions of persecution. Although the prisoner was sane on many subjects, her
overall mentality suffered from a paranoiac condition.

As the witness came to the end of his recital, counsel
Adrian Riker read a ten-thousand-word statement which

summed up Dr. Cotton's entire testimony. At one point where her distrust of lawyers was referred to, Mrs. Martin interjected, "I never had a lawyer in this whole case." Again, the word "murder" brought a loud outcry; "Murder? Murder? I never committed murder, never, never any more than the judge. Why I never murdered a fly." Still a third objection saw Mrs. Martin wring her hands and weep. On each occasion the judge was able to quiet her, the last time by saying, "You have taught school, Mrs. Martin. Did you allow your pupils to speak out at all times?" "I did, if I could get the truth that way," the prisoner answered, and subsided.

The end of Riker's long declaration turned it into a hypothetical question, asking if its object could be considered sane. Dr. Cotton replied that such a person as the one described would be technically insane, unable to distinguish right and wrong, incompetent to aid in her defense on a murder charge.

"Will she ever, in your opinion, become better?" asked Judge Ten Eyck.

"She will not," said the witness. "Her condition is progressive due to abnormal personality."

Acting Police Surgeon Walter Washington followed Dr. Cotton to the stand and gave a similar account. During his testimony Mrs. Martin indulged herself once more with a perspicacious sally that drew smiles and laughter from all in the courtroom.

He was engaged by defense counsel in February to examine the prisoner, said Dr. Washington. Mrs. Martin had immediately flown into a passion of weeping and denial of guilt, assailing lawyer Franklin Fort as "foxy, a liar, pigheaded, and a traitor." She had told of her grandiose ideas for the creative supervision of her entire family and boasted of her intimate connections with rich and important people.

Mrs. Martin was not at present a danger to anyone, Dr. Washington concluded, nor was she willfully untruthful. Because of her mental condition, however, she could not give an accurate account of anything, and the sum of her delusions made her unqualified to wage a defense in the present case.

"You know, many sane clients are suspicious of their lawyers," special counsel Louis Hood remarked on cross-examination.

"I suppose so," said Dr. Washington.

"And you know, lawyers have sometimes done dishonorable things."

"I suppose so."

"Mrs. Martin considers she is sane."

"A common delusion of insane people. She says she is sane and the rest of the world insane."

"I do," quipped Mrs. Martin. "I mean specifically in Essex County."

When the gaiety evoked by this remark subsided, Judge Ten Eyck announced that the third defense physician would not appear. Dr. William Mabon, superintendent of the Metropolitan State Hospital for the Insane at Ward's Island, was also to give a finding of insanity. The absent witness, who had figured in the sensational Harry Thaw murder trial, was preoccupied with trouble at his institution where certain supplies were missing and his presence was needed for the investigation. As a consequence, the defense decided to rest its case.

27

ON MONDAY, NOVEMBER 27, one whole year after the tragic death of Ocey Snead, the prosecution began its case to prove Caroline Martin sane and able to stand trial for her daughter's murder. When the judge set a new date, January 9, 1911, for that trial, the prisoner took exception.

"It will take a lawyer some time to study my case," she said. "And none of them will work during the holidays. Not one."

"If I appoint a lawyer for you, I will name one who will work during the holidays," answered Judge Ten Eyck.

"Will this testimony go to the jury in the other case?"

"Not one word."

The judge's reply was satisfactory to her. Police Surgeon J. Henry Clark took the stand as the first prosecution witness. Accompanied by Dr. Christopher Beling and Dr. William Hicks, he had paid many visits to Mrs. Martin in jail. His conclusion was that she was sane. He related conversations which to him seemed reasoned and measured. Her lawyer had told her, she once said to Dr. Clark, that Prosecutor Mott had proof that she was seen murdering Ocey Snead, and that her only hope of avoiding conviction was in a plea of insanity. Checking, Dr. Clark learned that defense counsel Beasley actually made this statement. Hence, she was not delusional in repeating it. Similarly, she said her sisters had wanted to make her out insane while actually she considered herself the "sanest woman in America." Again there was a basis for this in fact, for at one time there had been family discussions about having her committed. Clark said the prisoner's behavior in court, which he held was not "boisterous" but "emotional," did not make him change his mind about her sanity.

The prisoner's talk of persecution by Wilbur Mott, the treachery of Franklin Fort, and the girl spy in prison was also not delusional since there was some data, however misinterpreted, backing it up. References to attending Vanderbilt receptions and breakfasting with Pierpont Morgan were not grotesquely extravagant but just family pride and boastfulness, again with some ground in fact. As for the assertion that Mrs. Martin was unbalanced because she had allegedly mentioned suicide, any person of pride who had spent almost a year in jail might understandably think of suicide.

Several times during the afternoon, when Louis Hood and Dr. Clark engaged in profound analysis of what constituted delusions, Mrs. Martin took little catnaps. Greatly refreshed, she would follow the ensuing dialogue closely, allowing herself an occasional comment. At one point, as Hood and Dr. Clark were trying to reconcile a point of interest, she said, "I would put those two boys in my ambiguic class." Later she demanded the word "equitable" be changed to "equable," declaring, "I pride myself on my English. I would rather be convicted and electrocuted than use bad English." At another moment, as they tried to define pre-senile delusional insanity, she blurted out, "Any crazy woman would get well on a chance to get out of jail, but I'm not crazy." When Dr. Clark said he thought she was in better mental condition now than eight years ago, she teasingly charged him with flattery.

"She is not untidy now," Dr. Clark pursued. "She does not throw money around."

"Because I haven't any to throw," Mrs. Martin called out,

much to the amusement of the spectators. When Dr. Clark had finished, she asked to speak and that request was granted.

"I didn't know that Italian girl was a spy," she said, referring to the fellow prisoner earlier mentioned, Mary Di John. "I gave her twenty-five cents to take a letter by dictation to Mr. Mott. Later there was a hullaballoo in the office and Mr. Mott demanded to know about this girl and the letter. I didn't say she was a spy but I did say that she stole my mother's letters."

To close the day's testimony, Dr. William Hicks, long connected with the Essex County Hospital for the Insane, said that in his view Mrs. Martin was sometimes close to the borderline of insanity but not actually insane. Her behavior, he felt, was that of a neurasthenic, not a madwoman.

Dr. Christopher Beling, a nerve and brain specialist with the insane asylum at Morris Plains, took the stand on Friday, December 2. The final prosecution witness, he gave the most elaborate explanation to date of Mrs. Martin's behavior, which he viewed as peculiar and eccentric, but definitely sane. She had given him, said Dr. Beling, a cogent account of Ocey Snead's death, which she attributed to a suicide pact between Ocey and her Aunt Virginia. In other matters, instead of being delusional, her beliefs had a substantive foundation.

"My daughter died from an overdose of morphine," he quoted the prisoner as saying. "She took too much, went into the bath, and died. She had talked of it for a year. We humored her and temporized and thought that when we moved out to East Orange she had lost the idea. Ocey began taking morphine following the birth of her first child, and her Aunt Virginia also took morphine for her neuralgia. Virginia started taking it after she lost the school in Christiansburg. She was despondent about that. The morphine was kept on a stand and used as other people use cologne. Both women wanted to die. They had a suicide pact between them. Mr. Mott has a letter that proves it."

Mrs. Martin was aware of and candid about the vagaries of her own mind, said Dr. Beling. Her loquacity she attributed to years of teaching and lecturing which developed the habit of freeing the mind. Her periodic displays of temper she related to physical symptoms, to pressures on the brain which made her first violent and then remorseful. She had denied all use and knowledge of hypnosis, saying, "Men should be allowed to settle the problems of mysterious science."

Often, said Dr. Beling, Mrs. Martin's remarks were to be taken as she had intended them, tongue in cheek, rather than literally. One day when he asked her where she was, she had replied, "Heaven," then had flown into a rage and demanded to be tried by a jury of women. Asked if she was afraid of death she said, "When you see us at the electric chair, you will see me smiling and with my head up. The Lord giveth his beloved sleep. When a woman who is sixty-five years of age is of no use to her family, nor to people in suffering, she should be Oslerized." The reference was to a suggestion once made by Sir William Osler, the Canadian physician and teacher of medicine, that all men over sixty be chloroformed.

Mrs. Martin's alleged paranoid behavior was usually related to actual fact, the specialist went on. In the case of the girl prisoner whom Mrs. Martin accused of spying on her, there was such a mitigating circumstance. Mrs. Martin said the girl stole letters from her. In the past, John Gebhardt, deputy United States marshal of New York, had once served a process on her nephew, Fletcher Snead, by means of a decoy letter. It was therefore no delusion to feel the mails were being used to trap her, and to offer the girl gifts if she would come over to her side. Similarly, her references to persecution by the family had substance. Testimony of her sister Bessie, who had wished to have her committed, should as a consequence be largely discounted.

The masses of clippings and documents which Mrs. Martin collected were gathered in order to write a great work of fiction, following therein the example of Charles Reade and many other writers who used the public print as inspiration for their own creation. "By coloring these episodes, they were to be compiled into a novel," she had told him. "If others could do it, I could. My people said I was crazy but I said they wouldn't think so when I sold my eighty-thousand-dollar novel." In point of fact, said Dr. Beling, Mrs. Martin's extensive reading had given her a comprehensive and remarkable vocabulary.

"Is there anything unusual about her language?" he was asked.

"Purely automatic, like your own," Mrs. Martin interjected, beginning a series of interruptions.

"What is your overall opinion of Mrs. Martin's mind?" the judge continued.

"If insanity is a mental disorder due to brain disease, she is not insane. Rather than breaking down, since 1893 her mind has improved. She is competent to advise with counsel, and has refused to tell things when advised not to. There is no evidence of marked impairment of judgment or of delusions. At worst, there is evidence of bad judgment and peculiarities difficult to explain. Bad judgment, I might say, is illustrated by isolated cases. Impaired judgment is judgment that is bad all the time. Mrs. Martin's mind is normal for one of her age, environment, and upbringing. Her condition does not tally with any known form of insanity."

"He's a foreigner," Mrs. Martin cut short the statement. "He can't judge an American."

"Do you want him to testify that you're crazy?" the annoyed Judge Ten Eyck asked.

"No, I want him to tell only the truth."

The interchange led the prisoner into one of her by now familiar tirades, a shouting, sobbing denunciation of the prosecution, the insurance companies, politicians. When a constable approached to calm her, Mrs. Martin fought furiously, screamed, then collapsed and was carried from the courtroom.

After a recess, on her promise to refrain from creating disturbances, the hearing resumed. Dr. Beling was asked if Mrs. Martin's habit of buying new clothing rather than washing soiled garments was not strange. The physician admitted this did not appear to show the best judgment.

"It all depends on laundry prices," commented Mrs. Martin, and this time the judge, too, joined in the mirth.

"Do you not find Mrs. Martin's outbursts in court an evidence of mental imbalance?"

"The circumstances of the case warrant these exhibitions," Dr. Beling said in concluding his testimony. "Mrs. Martin is highly emotional and keenly feels her position. She has been in jail almost a year, is worn out with her ordeal, unrepresented by counsel, and in fear that evidence is sought at this hearing to be used against her at a future trial. Under this strain she naturally gives way at times. And yet I call attention to the fact that she has made frequent pertinent remarks. She doesn't seem to appreciate the reasons for this hearing. Yet she is amenable to the orders of this court. In the hearing before the experts and the court, when all of us questioned her, she worked herself up to an emotional state in which she seemed fearful of the subjects of our questioning, accentuated by her declared absence or lack of friends. Still, she calmed down very soon. There is nothing unnatural in her behavior in the court."

On Wednesday, November 30, both sides were given three hours to sum up their arguments. For the prosecution, Louis Hood said that if delusions are falsified beliefs arising spontaneously, Mrs. Martin was not delusional. Her tirades were only a form of stage fright; great suspense had led to incoherence but not insanity. She was, after all, in the horrible predicament where if sane she would be tried for murder, if insane sent to an asylum.

"The truth is, she needs hospital treatment," Hood told the court. "Although she declares she is sane, still she has no faith in the purpose of the prosecution in trying to establish her sanity. This is understandable."

Each person's sanity must be judged in the context of his own background and environment, Hood maintained, detailing at length how the prisoner had adapted well enough to survive in various situations for many years, a sign of sanity.

"The people of Constantinople some time ago rushed out with bells to drive away the beast that was swallowing the sun during an eclipse," the special counsel ended his summation. "They acted in unison, according to environment and teaching. In all people are differences in the process of reasoning and in their conclusions, but in the case of the Turks one could not call their act an evidence of a delusion. If there were pre-senile delusions in the case of Mrs. Martin, then she would not have had the faculty to teach school for many years and the delusions now would be so fixed, systematized, and fantastic that there would be no hesitation on the part of any doctor to call her insane. She is sane."

For the defense, Chauncy Beasley summed up the many instances in which he viewed Mrs. Martin's behavior as delusional — her talk of familiarity with Hetty Green, Helen Gould, Andrew Carnegie, and others she did not know at all or knew only in passing, her belief that the principals in the

case were all profiting by her predicament, her unorthodox
behavior with banker Vaughan and many others. She was
clearly outside the pale of rationality, he insisted, and added
that alienists were disposed to be "prejudiced."

"I believe you could have decided this case without the
testimony of alienists, using solely the testimony of lay witnesses and your own observation of Mrs. Martin," Beasley
told the judge. "With all due respect to these experts, the
history of insanity cases shows that alienists are prejudiced
witnesses. In their particular quests they go too far. I prefer
the testimony of laymen."

On this last day of the hearing, Mrs. Martin gave the court
a final salvo of interruptions and attacks. Each mention of
the word "murder" elicited an outcry, with the judge more
annoyed than ever before.

"I am not going to sit in this case six months," he said
exasperatedly at one point. "I've given you too much latitude
altogether. Now you've got to keep still."

"But I'm accused and have no attorney," said the prisoner,
swinging into an old refrain.

"You are not on trial, and you will have to let this testimony proceed. Whether you are crazy or not you know
enough to keep still when you are told. Now I don't want
any more remarks."

In her attacks, Mrs. Martin had sometimes lifted her hood
to peer out at the judge and evaluate his reaction. If it was
mild, she continued to use her peephole. If stern, she swiftly
replaced the hood, somewhat in the manner of a naughty
child testing to see how far she could go. Now the judge's
sharp rebuke sent her fairly collapsing into her seat, where
she wept quietly into a black handkerchief. She listened in
silence to the last words of Hood and to short remarks by
Wilbur Mott, who called the Beasley criticism of alienists
"ungracious."

The public hearing was over, but on Monday, December 5, Judge Ten Eyck received the prisoner alone in his chamber from 9:45 until twelve noon. "I told her I would give her this chance," he explained later. "The visit afforded me an opportunity to observe her under normal circumstances. In the court she was under great mental stress."

28

THE INQUIRY HAD LASTED the better part of a month. For a week after its close Judge Ten Eyck made an intensive review of the testimony and the various technical questions involved. On Friday, December 9, he made his conclusions public and ordered them filed with the city clerk. Mrs. Martin, he wrote, was sane within the meaning of the statute, competent to advise counsel and assist in the preparation of a defense.

Citing prior cases, Ten Eyck stated that in an inquiry such as the present, the prisoner might be insane to some degree and yet judged capable of making a rational defense. In coming to a decision, he had taken into consideration views of members of the family that Mrs. Martin was insane. These could not be given controlling weight since the family did not act at any time to verify their views, did not have her examined by medical men, or make serious efforts to have her placed in an institution. As for other lay witnesses, their testimony could not be fully credited since without so intending they would incline toward a natural bias or prejudice. It was common knowledge that many persons had been committed to an asylum by well-meaning but mistaken friends. Even honest and competent experts could be wrong. However, insofar as expert testimony consisted not of mere opinion but of scientific knowledge, of experience and writings relating to classifiable symptoms of mental disorder, it could be of the highest value, much more than that of any lay witness. Insanity had some technical basis behind it, and hence this must be investigated.

The two petitioners, wrote the judge, maintained that Mrs. Martin was suffering from a progressive disease of the brain of a paranoid type and that she had the essential symptoms of pre-senile delusional insanity, a recent classification of a rare type of insanity. Only twelve cases had been so diagnosed in the last ten years. These had the following distinguishing characteristics: (1) impairment of judgment, (2) emotional irritability, and (3) unsystematized and changing or unstable delusions of suspicion, beginning with hypochondriacal delusions of various hysterical kinds, later becoming fantastic and senseless. The petitioner's experts agree that all three of these conditions must exist in order to constitute this particular form of insanity. To establish their contention they cited statements made by Mrs. Martin in various jail interviews and her prior conduct, especially since 1902, the date of her retirement as principal of a public school in New York.

That she had emotional irritation and probably impaired judgment, certainly bad judgment in some matters, was admitted by the state, which claimed, however, that these symptoms were probably caused by cerebral neurasthenia, possibly due to an internal disorder and not to insanity. The symptoms had existed at least as far back as 1885, and if they were due to insanity they would now be so pronounced that no alienist could fail to diagnose the case as one of insanity; whereas, in the judgment of the state's experts, Mrs. Martin was actually in better mental condition now than in the years between 1902 and 1909.

That Mrs. Martin did suffer from physical trouble sufficient to cause neurasthenia seemed to be plain, said Judge Ten Eyck. That this might be the cause of some emotional irritation and some degree of impaired judgment in a sane person of her age also seemed plain. Therefore, the turning point of the case as to insanity in general hinged on the presence or absence of insane delusions. These would have to be present in persistent quantity, as many sane persons had some of them. The written analysis of Judge Ten Eyck on this point was extensive:

"If Mrs. Martin's habit of collecting newspapers, clothing, etc. constituted this grave symptom, it cannot be said that it supports the theory of pre-senile delusional insanity, so far as any author has yet written on the subject. In the absence of other evidence of serious mental disease, which would in such case be easily perceived, it is reasonable to ascribe this habit, standing alone, so far as the collection of newspapers is concerned, to her stated intent to use them as data for the writing of a book, and her expectation to do so after retirement. As to the clothing and other things, with a full knowledge of the facts, and in the absence of any other things, or a full absence of any other evidence of well-marked mental disease, the inference that it indicates insane collectionism is not, in my judgment, justified.

"Her beliefs, as shown by the interviews in the jail, are fixed and not changeable, and in this respect do not correspond with the symptoms of pre-senile delusional insanity; also in my judgment, they have sufficient foundation in fact to justify her beliefs as to the main features; the details, so far as they are not so justified, may be well ascribed to her habit of embellishment and her naturally imaginative mind. As to these matters, while her statements and beliefs were not in many instances founded upon facts, or premises which ought to be recognized by any ordinary well-informed person as sufficient, still taking into consideration her natural temperament, her age, her serious impairment of physical condition, her unfamiliarity with legal and business matters of this kind, her environment and situation, being without personal counsel, her arrest on the charge of the murder of her own daughter, her extradition and reflection upon her family name, the activity of the prosecution and detectives to obtain evidence against her, the hostility of the insurance companies, her fear, the action of Judge Phlegar and her relatives and former attorney in the matter of the assignment of the insurance policies against her emphatic protest; the written statement made by Miss Wardlaw and refusal of her attorneys to surrender it; the allegations of fraud in the extradition proceedings contained in the habeas corpus petition; all these things might well account for statements and beliefs, insofar as they are her real beliefs, and not merely things she says were told her and she does not pretend to know about, there is in this enough of a basis of fact to justify one in her position to hold these beliefs, and to at least take them out of the category of insane delusions arising either spontaneously in her mind or without any possible reasonable basis of fact to rest upon consistent with the exercise of any degree of rational reasoning power.

"As to her conduct between 1902 and 1909, some acts of peculiar conduct are shown, which taken alone, are explicable only on the theory either that there was some degree of impaired judgment, or that at these particular periods she was suffering from temporary attacks of mental disorder of some kind. During the same period, however, she traveled extensively, did some teaching, was consulted by Miss Wardlaw about the management of the schools of Murfreesboro and Christiansburg, made a contract with Miss Van Wagenen in relation to her daughter's education, borrowed large sums from Mr. Elliot, a New York attorney, and assigned to him her pension as lateral security, which he still holds.

"Without a full knowledge of all the factors accompanying her peculiar actions and possible reasons therefor, it cannot be said that in themselves they show with any degree of certitude whether they were due to insanity or to some other cause. It does not appear that she had any insane delusions at that time. The colored women who testified were evidently with her, as a rule, only while Miss Wardlaw was busy with the school. I cannot believe that their evidence is conclusive as to the personal care she received. It may be all they know about it, but I have no doubt that she did, in fact, eat and was bathed and attended to in a reasonable manner by Miss Wardlaw or Mrs. Snead, probably, in the absence of these servants. On the face of it, it seems to me clear that their testimony cannot be taken as at all conclusive as to the life and habits of Mrs. Martin during the period covered by their testimony. The fact that counsel, who admittedly were not to represent her at the trial, may have had difficulty or found it impossible to get from her facts they thought important is far from conclusive on this point.

"Mrs. Martin's conduct in court, while altogether unusual and in some instances hysterical, in my judgment did not indicate insanity. It did show excitability, irritability, and bad judgment. It also showed she had a good deal of physical and mental endurance, a keen alert mind, a remarkably good memory, both for remote and recent events, a pretty clear comprehension of the whole case for a woman laboring under severe strain, and forcible and accurate power of expression. In several instances, where I thought at the time she surely must be wrong, it was soon proved that she was right. Also, there is no evidence that during her long confinement in jail, her conduct has been that of an insane person;

there is evidence that during this period her conduct was normal.

"It would be practically impossible and useless to go more extensively into the evidence in this case and state all that might be said, bearing on the substance, and to discuss fully the voluminous evidence in the case. My conclusion of the whole case is that the only reasonable view to adopt is that the evidence entirely fails to overcome the presumption that the defendant is sane at this time, and that at all events Mrs. Martin is capable of understanding her position, the nature of the charge against her, and of consulting rationally with counsel and preparing her defense. I will certify that I find, as a result of this inquiry, that the said Caroline B. Martin is not insane and should not be discharged from the Essex County jail, where she is now held awaiting trial, nor removed therefrom to any insane asylum as an insane person."

Having so often denounced the perfidy of lawyers, Mrs. Martin could have derived only grim satisfaction from news brought to her jail cell at about the same time as the judge's decision. One of her team of counsellors, Robert Haire, had been indicted by a grand jury for the attempted subornation of a witness in another case. Awaiting trial for grand larceny, prisoner John Rodgers, in New York's Tombs Prison, said Haire and his partner had several times proposed a scheme to get him to give false testimony. Haire pleaded not guilty.

No such slight charge faced Mrs. Martin. As a result of Judge Ten Eyck's ruling, she and her sister would now be tried for murder.

29

THE LONG-AWAITED TRIAL of Mrs. Caroline Martin and Mrs. Mary Snead finally began on Monday, January 9, 1911. To the consternation of spectators it ended on the same day when defense counsel withdrew Mrs. Martin's plea of not guilty and entered a plea of guilty to the charge of manslaughter. After arduous and costly preparations for a long trial, the attorneys had made a radical switch in strategy.

Pathos underlined the day's proceedings in court. Mary Snead sat in silence, and even Mrs. Martin seemed to be drained of her usual vitality. She sat quietly while a conference was held in the judge's chambers between Ten Eyck, Wilbur Mott, Frank S. Sommer, and Samuel Kalish, the latter two assigned by the court for the defense. As soon as the session began, Kalish addressed the court, announcing the change in plea. The following colloquy then occurred:

PROSECUTOR MOTT: Since counsel, Your Honor, has indicated willingness to plead *non vult* to manslaughter . . .

MRS. MARTIN: Involuntary, please, sir.

MOTT: Manslaughter, madam.

MRS. MARTIN: I didn't do anything.

MOTT: I have given the matter the most careful consideration and now advise Your Honor to accept the plea. I am influenced in so doing by the consideration of her age.

JUDGE TEN EYCK: There is no such plea as *non vult* to involuntary manslaughter. I can only accept *non vult* to the charge of manslaughter.

MRS. MARTIN: How can it be manslaughter, when she was just a lovely little girl?

COUNSEL SAMUEL KALISH: We believe that there is no moral responsibility, but that there may be legal responsibility.

MRS. MARTIN: This is too much for me.

MOTT: Mrs. Martin, your counsel have advised me that you wish to make this plea. Do you?

MRS. MARTIN: You men may understand all this. I don't. I didn't do anything. I didn't do anything to my daughter. Oh, I don't know what to do. I suppose this man Kalish is just not quite so cruel as the rest of them, but I tell you I never did anything to my daughter. I'd rather go to the electric chair ten thousand times and get rid of this hypocrisy. I did nothing more than you may have done to your daughter, Judge. I am in the hands of Jerseymen, and I have never seen such men since God made man.

KALISH: She accepts your plea, Your Honor. I am authorized to say so for her.

The maximum penalty for manslaughter was ten years, said the judge, announcing he would pass sentence after further review of the case. As he left the bench, Mrs. Martin protested that she thought she was to be given her freedom.

"Can I go home now?" she asked attorney Sommer, but the only reply was a deputy sheriff's strong arm leading her back to jail.

30

MANY OBSERVERS EXPECTED THAT IN PASSING SENTENCE Judge Ten Eyck would order the prisoner, due to her age and mental infirmities, to serve time in a state mental institution rather than a prison. As usual in the baffling case of the bathtub tragedy, the expected did not materialize.

The judge's demeanor was grave as he opened court on Monday, January 23, 1911. Before passing sentence, he listened to an appeal for clemency from Samuel Kalish. The attorney's argument was still another shocker which threw new light on the death of Ocey Snead.

"Mrs. Martin has said that Ocey Snead was ill the night before she died and lay all that night with her head in her mother's lap," said Kalish. "She has since admitted that she had given Ocey morphine that night to induce sleep, as she had done on other occasions. When she saw how the drug had affected Ocey she put the young woman in cold water in the bathtub in the hope of reviving her. When she finally realized Ocey's condition she became greatly alarmed and went back to New York half crazed over the result of the treatment she had given her daughter."

Never had Mrs. Martin given a coherent story about the precise manner and time of Ocey Snead's death, said the attorney, nor had she ever admitted anything that would show criminal intent. He discounted the theory that the sisters had plotted against the girl's life for her insurance, and closed his plea with references to the high standing of the Wardlaw family.

Wilbur Mott replied that he was opposed to any leniency of sentence. As the investigating prosecutor he had become more and more convinced that a deliberate crime had been committed; it seemed to him the old women "hung over the body of Ocey like buzzards over a dying dog." The fresh revelations by Kalish did not change his views.

"If that theory is accepted," he concluded, referring to the morphine dosage, "then the moral turpitude of Mrs. Martin is still evident, for she was like a man in an automobile who after running over a child puts on high speed and flees. She fled when she realized the condition of her daughter and left her to her fate."

"I am innocent in the sight of God," Mrs. Martin interpolated. "I am as innocent as Judge Ten Eyck or Mr. Mott. I have done absolutely nothing to injure my daughter, absolutely nothing."

"Mrs. Martin," the judge began his sentencing statement, "I have given your counsel opportunity to be heard in your behalf in this matter of sentence to be imposed in this case, and I have listened to what they have had to say, as well as to what the prosecutor stated, and I am now ready to pronounce sentence. You were indicted together with your two sisters for murder in the case of the death of Ocey Snead. Immediately upon your daughter's death, under circumstances which pointed strongly to the conclusion that while under the care of yourself and your sisters she was a victim of criminal homicide, you fled to New York and were brought back under extradition proceedings. Very soon after this, counsel for the defendants took various proceedings, which if successful would have precluded any trial upon the indictments. These included habeas corpus, an injunction suit to restrain the prosecution from using the letters and documents which had been seized in New York, and finally an investigation as to your sanity . . ."

"We wanted every document brought out," said Mrs. Martin. "We did not want to hide anything."

"Mrs. Martin, I wish to inform you that the time for you to speak is past, and that you must keep quiet and not interrupt while I am disposing of this case. I will not tolerate any interruptions whatever.

"After all these had been decided adversely," the judge continued, "and there was no further hope of preventing trial, acting upon the advice of able counsel who represented you, you offered a plea of *non vult* to the charge of manslaughter. In view of the circumstances which then appeared, this plea was accepted. It amounts to a plea of guilty for the purpose of this proceeding.

"It is probable that the entire facts leading up to this mysterious death will never be known. Neither you nor Mrs. Snead have ever made a full and complete statement at any time. From their own statements, made in open court, it appeared that most of the information your counsel had as to the facts was derived from evidence in the possession of the prosecutor, and their theory as to how the death probably occurred was, as they stated, largely conjecture. There were, however, sufficiently undisputed facts to show conclusively that you were at least guilty of manslaughter.

"I am convinced that you have willfully refused to make a full statement of the facts to your counsel. It appeared in the sanity proceedings that there was one statement made by Miss Wardlaw to her counsel. What it contained I do not know, but assume that you must have discovered the purport of it, for you at once demanded that he should surrender it, and ever since his refusal to do so you have made extravagant and, I believe, unjust charges against him, which reflected also upon Miss Wardlaw.

"The facts, as they were then known to the prosecution, showed a strong probability that a criminal homicide of some kind had been committed, and an indictment for murder was properly found. Nothing was known until very recently which would indicate that it might be a case of manslaughter rather than murder. Instead of frankly stating that you had yourself, with innocent intent, administered to your daughter a large dose of morphine, which you have recently stated to be true, you constantly denied that you were present when your daughter died, and insisted that you knew nothing of her death until you read of it in the New York papers.

"Some of the important facts in the case are: the strange conduct and writings of yourself and your sisters during the period preceding your coming to East Orange, relating to your daughter, her illness, the large insurance upon her life, and your financial troubles; the knowledge which you say you had of a suicide pact between her and Miss Wardlaw; her frequent use of morphine; the strange disappearance of your daughter's husband; your knowledge, according to your own statement, that she was in a morbid state of mind and was engaged in writing a book to be called *The Beautiful Suicide;* her writing of numerous 'suicide notes,' many of which were found in your possession; the fact that you and your sisters brought your daughter to an unfurnished house in East Orange and kept her there for several days without proper food; the report by Miss Wardlaw of her death, and discovery of her body by the police about eighteen hours after death with one of the suicide notes pinned to her clothing; the futile attempt to create an impression that she had drowned herself while bathing, she having been then in a state of profound narcosis from morphine and unable to bathe herself; your flight, taking the morphine bottle, and hiding in various hotels in New York, under different names; your false denial of having been in East Orange . . ."

At this mention of East Orange, Mrs. Martin buried her head in her arms and shook convulsively. Recovering, she straightened in her chair and began a tirade as pathetic as it was unsparing.

"I never denied being in East Orange in my life, never," she insisted. "This is a series of lies by men against a mother, an innocent mother who has done nothing to her child but love her and care for her, by men that wouldn't keep her from starving but who take the taxpayer's money for black-ening her name — my baby's name. I have done nothing to my child. I have done nothing to anybody living or dead, except love them and strive to help them all my life. What the judge is saying is based upon the lies of men who do not know a mother's heart. . . ."

Rapping hard, Judge Ten Eyck declared a recess. Wholly collapsed in her chair, Mrs. Martin was carried out of the room by two attendants, her protests audible until the door of the judge's private chamber closed behind her. "Oh, God, that men should do this to women," her shrill voice was heard to say. "Oh, that they should seek to blacken the name of my fair child. Oh, that they should blacken, blacken, blacken. I never did give her any morphine in my life. I never gave anybody morphine. I never stated so to anybody living!"

The brief respite calmed Mrs. Martin. She returned to the courtroom where the judge continued by saying, "In the face of these facts you insisted that everyone concerned was en-gaged in a conspiracy against you, charging that this state's witnesses were paid perjurers and that the public press was subsidized to misrepresent you. Many of these matters, without explanation, would tend strongly to justify the belief that your daughter's death was due to something more than mere criminal negligence. The only explanation is that which may be inferred from your own recent statement. If that is true, and I have no reason to believe that it is not, it might in connection with some of the other facts above re-ferred to warrant two different conclusions, one consistent with innocent intent.

"The former view is somewhat difficult of adoption, but in view of the fact that there has been much strange and ab-normal conduct on your part in recent years pertaining to other matters, it may be that your strange conduct in this case is capable of explanation upon some theory other than that involving criminal intent, and may justify the theory stated by your counsel that after giving your daughter the morphine, you may have placed her in the water in an attempt to revive her, and failing in that you fled on account of fear."

"I never did give her any morphine in my life," Mrs. Martin almost screamed. "I never gave anybody morphine. I never stated so to anybody living!"

"Under any possible theory, however," the judge went firmly on, "I cannot under all the facts regard this case otherwise than as one involving great moral turpitude. Public interest requires that crimes involving death by the insidious means of poisoning should, in practically every case, be severely punished. The peculiar facts here shown, and your recent history in general, indicate that a sentence should be imposed which will be sufficient to assure that there will hereafter be no danger of injury to anyone which might result from further peculiar conduct on your part.

"The sentence of the court in this case is that you be confined in the New Jersey State Prison for the term of seven years and from thence until the costs are paid."

As the severe statement came to an end, Mrs. Martin sat as if transfixed, her features not discernible through heavy black veils but her face directed squarely at the judge.

"This is not done to justify Governor Hughes or Governor Fort," she exclaimed. "It is done to justify Mr. Mott and those who have helped him. God knows it is not because I deserve it. I don't deserve it. Oh, God have mercy. Have mercy."

The piteous appeal moved everyone within sound of the prisoner's voice, and the protests of innocence continued until she was placed into a van to return to jail. There she could contemplate the bleak future. If able to serve the full term imposed, Mrs. Martin would be seventy-two years old on release.

31

THE AGED PRISONER SPENT THE SUCCEEDING DAYS in putting her affairs in order. A short time earlier, she had packed several barrelfuls of newspapers and sent them to a warehouse. Now she filled eight additional cases with clippings and other effects and stored them in the Knickerbocker Company's Manhattan warehouse. She was able to pay the charges out of her own resources. The public school pension which she had assigned to lawyer Maxwell Elliott had reverted back to her after his loans were covered and now netted her almost a hundred dollars a month.

In these final days in Newark there was little communication between Mrs. Martin and her sister. She had protested when many months earlier Mary Snead had been moved to a separate tier of the jail. She needed her, she said, to manicure her nails, to read the papers for her, and to write her letters. On Wednesday, February 8, the convicted prisoner bade Mary an unemotional good-bye.

Warden Richard McGuinness had told her it was time to leave for Trenton a day ahead of schedule. From Mrs. Martin, known for her tempestuous and articulate nature, there issued no further demonstration. "It might just as well come now as any other time," she said simply.

In a slight resurgence of that strong pride for which she was also known, she declined to be taken to the Market

Street station in a prison van, hiring instead a carriage which she paid for out of her own funds. At 3:23 in the afternoon the Pennsylvania Railroad's train began its trip, the prisoner riding in a private car accompanied by the warden and his wife, along with Constable Philip McManus.

With no prying eyes to stare at her, Mrs. Martin lifted her veils and looked in wonder at the passing scenery. The journey was otherwise uneventful. On reaching Trenton, Mrs. Martin said good-bye to the McGuinnesses. All wept at the parting, for in the thirteen long months just past the warden and his wife had come to know the prisoner well, to develop an admiration for the finer qualities of her mind and a sympathy for her plight. They were aware, too, that a fresh blow awaited her. Prison rules would require that she wear regulation clothing and shed the black cape, the black gloves, and the dark veils which seemed so much a part of her very being.

32

THE DEPARTURE OF MRS. MARTIN allowed the retiring Mary Snead a fleeting moment in the limelight. On Thursday, February 8, she appeared in court and was given her freedom. The motion to quash the indictment against her was made by Wilbur Mott. The prosecutor explained that since Mrs. Martin had pleaded *non vult* to manslaughter, and as a matter of law there was no accessory to manslaughter, it followed that Mary Snead could not be brought to trial as an accessory to her sister's action.

Leaving the courtroom with her was Albert Snead, her

son, who had come from Colorado to be at her side. A pleas-
ant-looking, unassuming young man in his early thirties, he
gave a statement to the press.

"I am glad to have my mother vindicated in this way,
without the necessity of her going through the unpleasant-
ness of a court trial," he said. "However, knowing as I do the
nobility of my mother's nature, and believing also in her innocence, I have never for a moment had the slightest fear
that the trial, if it had taken place, would have resulted
other than in her complete vindication. And I believe I am
safe in saying not only for myself but for everyone who has
ever known her that there is not one whose faith in my
mother's innocence and in the purity of her character has
been shaken in the least by the accusations that were made
against her, and on account of which she has been held in
custody.

"The dropping of the indictment did not come as a surprise to me, as I was personally assured by the prosecutor
more than two weeks ago that he was ready to release my
mother at any time thereafter that she might request it.
However, on account of the pitiable condition, both physical
and mental, of her sister, Mrs. Martin, my mother requested
to be allowed to remain temporarily with Mrs. Martin in
order to minister to her needs. It was for this reason that my
mother's case was not disposed of before this time.

"I do not know where my brother is," Albert continued,
answering rumors that Fletcher Snead was also in Newark.
"He has not written to me nor to his mother. When he is
ready to make himself known, we probably will be notified.

"Mrs. Martin expected to be taken to Trenton Thursday
and was making her preparations accordingly," he went on
in explaining the apparent cold farewell between his mother
and her sister. "Then on Wednesday came notice from the
sheriff's office that Mrs. Martin was to be taken at once. This

gave less than an hour in which to complete preparations. Mrs. Martin thinks more of her papers and other effects than she does of her own life. Her inattention to my mother was due solely to her anxiety and excitement caused by that sudden notice. There never has been any ill feeling between them.

"We will stay here for some little time yet," he concluded. "Before long we expect to go to Trenton to see Mrs. Martin. We will do whatever we can for her comfort. While we feel that she is insane and should be in a sanitarium, we have not yet decided on any action save to do as much as possible for her comfort . . . My mother and I both believe her innocent of moral and physical wrong in this case, and because of her mental condition entertain for her the utmost pity and love."

After settling affairs in the city, Albert Snead took his mother with him to his Colorado ranch. In welcome obscurity she lived out her days, trying to forget the painful trauma that had darkened her days.

33

AT THE NEW JERSEY STATE PRISON IN TRENTON, the redoubtable Mrs. Martin still dared to dream the impossible dream, insisting on her innocence, telling the principal keeper of four new lawyers whom she had hired to search for legal loopholes, of Fletcher Snead who, like a knight errant of old, would surely come to rescue her from imprisonment and carry her away.

As the monotonous days went by, however, there was no real ray of hope. Under prison regulations Mrs. Martin was allowed to read books — and her cherished newspapers. She was put on a special diet, but even so her condition rapidly became feeble; she could not be given even light duties. Toward the end of the year she began to experience frequent attacks of stupor and after recovering would become hysterical. Finally these attacks became so severe that she was transferred to the State Hospital for the Insane, where needed medical facilities were more readily available.

Perhaps the move was a relief to Mrs. Martin. The same architect, John Haviland, had designed not only New York's Tombs Prison and Newark's Essex County Jail, but also the New Jersey State Prison at Trenton. At last she was out from under his gloomy shadow.

For more than a year, the illness was brought under control, only to begin anew. Old age and the harrowing experiences of prison had taken a severe toll. The once heavy-set frame of the prisoner turned skeletal. Early on Friday, June 20, 1913, stupor struck again, and Mrs. Martin fell unconscious. The following night she died. So greatly deteriorated was her body that it led to morbid speculation. Had she followed her sister Virginia's example and deliberately starved herself, or had she perhaps committed suicide by taking poison? An autopsy performed by County Physician Frank Scammell and Dr. Harry Cotton, the hospital's medical director, quieted these rumors. It showed that death had come from natural causes, from a fatty degeneration of the heart. With the shipment of the body to the South for burial, the state closed the books on one of the most bewildering cases in its history.

Death could only obscure for all time the actual circumstances of the passing of the beautiful Ocey Snead. Where did the truth lie, and what was falsehood? In that complex maze of testimony and documentation, what was real and what was illusory? If the case had been simply one of mental imbalance scarring a famous family, it would probably not have held the public's continuing interest. It was the extraordinary personalities of the Wardlaw sisters, the three women in black, which made it a spellbinder, rendering it ever multifaceted, leaving it always ambiguous.

34

INEVITABLY, THIS HISTORY in which conflicting elements are present in such abundance has several footnotes or epilogues. In October 1929, the *Genealogy of the Wardlaw Family* appeared, compiled by Joseph G. Wardlaw. Published in York, South Carolina, it made no mention of the famous case which afflicted the family twenty years earlier. It did, however, quote Judge David Lewis Wardlaw on a pertinent subject, family traits and heredity.

"I believe firmly in hereditary influence, not only upon bodily form, movements, appetites, but upon the moral propensities and feelings connected with these qualities, and upon all the mental facilities," the judge had written in 1872. "I believe these inherited qualities often disappear for one generation or more, and then reappear, so that often a descendant resembles as much an uncle or grandmother as a father or grandfather. Further, I believe that by free and judicious selection the human race might be so improved that a man of the new species would be as far above one of the present as a Caucasian is now above a gorilla."

On January 28, 1930, the bathtub murder mystery was briefly reopened when a cache of jewelry was found in a safe deposit box of Murfreesboro's First National Bank. Three loose diamonds and two diamond-studded brooches comprised the lot, contained in a small black bag. Pinned to a fingerless black mitt was a tag labeled *Miss Virginia Wardlaw.*

In East Orange, William O'Neill, now the town police chief, said he thought the sisters, when so desperately in need of money, must have forgotten about the jewelry. C. B. Bell, the bank's cashier, said he was ready to turn over the diamonds and brooches, valued at two thousand dollars, to their rightful owner.

Newspapers across the country publicized the discovery but no survivor of the once proud Wardlaw family appeared to make a claim. Fletcher Snead, it was learned, had drifted into a sparsely populated forest region of Canada's interior. Albert Snead had moved to California. As often happens in such cases, legal minions and creditors from days long past devoured the proceeds from sale of the jewelry. The bag and the black glove, last remnants of the three sisters, were burned. Curiously, in all the voluminous courtroom interrogations, in all the lengthy interviews with reporters, no one had ever asked the women the most obvious of questions — why did they wear black? Themselves a pattern in triplicate, they would surely have had a ready answer. Perhaps even two or three.

Acknowledgments

I AM PARTICULARLY GRATEFUL to the directors and staffs of the following institutions for so graciously making their materials available to me: the Essex County Hall of Records in Newark; the Newark Public Library, especially the New Jersey Room; the New York Historical Society; and the New York Public Library.

In addition to those court records available, information was gleaned from newspapers of the day, which gave lavish coverage to the case of the bathtub tragedy. Those consulted include: Newark's *Evening News, Evening Star,* and *Sunday Call;* New York's *World, Times, Herald, Evening Sun,* and *Daily Tribune.*

The *Genealogy of the Wardlaw Family,* compiled by Joseph G. Wardlaw, was referred to in the text. It was published in York, South Carolina, in 1929. *The Wardlaws in Scotland,* by John C. Gibson, was published in Edinburgh in 1912. Some of the facts helping to fill out Southern backgrounds were provided by *The Montgomery County Story 1776–1957,* edited by Charles W. Crush and published in 1957 under the sponsorship of that county's Board of Supervisors; and *A History of Rutherford County,* edited by Carlton C. Sims and published in 1947, one of a series of county histories written at the suggestion of the Tennessee Historical Commission. The *Industrial Directory of New Jersey* is compiled annually by that state's Bureau of Statistics.

Two books contain interesting accounts of the death of Ocey Snead. Alvin F. Harlow includes the case in his volume *Murders Not Quite Solved,* published by Julian Messner in 1938; and a briefer summary appears in Allen Churchill's lively *Pictorial History of the American Theatre*, published in 1964 by Holt, Rinehart and Winston.

Finally, a word of thanks to my friend Rita Senf for her help with the manuscript, and to Harry Sions for his thoughtful editing.

NORMAN ZIEROLD